D1058112

THE BOOK OF UNCOMMON PRAYER

The

BOOK

of

UNCOMMON

PRAYER

EDITED BY

CONSTANCE POLLOCK

& DANIEL POLLOCK

WORD PUBLISHING

DALLAS LONDON VANCOUVER MELBOURNE

WORD PUBLISHING

Book design by Mark McGarry
Set in Monotype Dante

LIBRARY OF CONGRESS CATALOGING-IN-PUBLICATION DATA
The book of uncommon prayer / edited by
Constance & Daniel Pollock
p. cm.
ISBN 0-8499-1335-7
1. Religious poetry. I. Pollock, Constance.
II. Pollock, Daniel.
PN6110.R4B56   1996
808.81'9382— dc20
96–43685
CIP

Printed in the United States of America

6 7 8 9 0 1 2   BVG   7 6 5 4 3 2 1

For our dear Jane

CONTENTS

The Book of Uncommon Prayer

INTRODUCTION

THE IDEA for this book was born about six weeks after our daughter Jane. Searching for special prayers to use at her baptism, we uncovered some lovely devotions in the works of Jane Austen, composed by the novelist herself. This aroused our curiosity about how other classic writers might have voiced their spiritual yearnings and relationship to God.

What treasures we found—from poets, playwrights, philosophers, novelists, and journalists. From some writers, we had expected eloquence on spiritual matters—the cleric John Donne, the mystic William Blake, the priest Gerard Manly Hopkins. Yet others amazed us. How could Edgar Allan Poe—brooding and self-destructive, the author of dark Gothic tales—pen such a tender tribute to Mary, the mother of Jesus? What impulse led Charles Dickens—who conjured a veritable carnival of humanity in his novels—to retell *The Life of Our Lord* in simple, accessible prose for his children, complete with prayers for their use? Again and again we found ourselves tapping into a rich vein of spirituality running through the lives and works of great literary artists—artists often considered strictly in secular terms.

Jane Austen, Charlotte and Emily Brontë, and Harriet Beecher Stowe, for example, wrote novels of enduring popularity. But they shared another experience—all were daughters of clergymen. Their prayers and devotions, perhaps, flowed naturally to their pens.

Other writers, however, traversed a rockier road. The Danish philosopher Søren Kierkegaard said of his conversion, "Christ came in through locked doors." Francis Thompson—a dissolute opium addict wandering the streets of London—tried to flee the "Hound of Heaven." But, to his salvation and our benefit, he succumbed to a religious faith he later described ecstatically and poetically. William Wordsworth, for many years content to worship God's perfection only in nature, returned to the Anglican Church for solace after the death of his brother.

Though separated by an ocean, two women born in the same year led remarkably parallel lives and arrived at a singular spiritual destination. Emily Dickinson and Christina Rossetti both ended love affairs and retreated into solitary existences. Yet their poetry reveals their private and passionate relationship with God that dominated their reclusive lives.

In similar ways, all the prayers, devotions, and meditations collected here offer glimpses into the inner lives of writers. Genius, on bended knee, reveals its humanity, its struggles, its joys. Though spread across centuries, these "uncommon prayers"—by Geoffrey Chaucer, Louisa May Alcott, Fyodor Dostoyevsky, Elizabeth Barrett Browning, and so many others—express emotions common to us all. The artists' gifts to us are the melodious phrase, the indelible image, the soothing rhythm, the piercing insight. They said it better, perhaps, and in doing so they quicken our intellects and innermost feelings, pointing us back to the divine source of their inspiration.

Because this is not a scholarly work, we have modernized archaic language and streamlined punctuation for easier apprehension. In some cases, we have excerpted longer works and contributed titles where there were none. While most of the writers speak for themselves, we have included prayers from characters they created for novels and plays.

The prayers are arranged alphabetically by author, while the index is designed to help the reader search by topic (such as Faith, Death, Praise, Thanksgiving). The biographical notes do not attempt to encapsulate a whole life, but rather highlight some important aspect of an author's spiritual journey.

CONSTANCE POLLOCK
& DANIEL POLLOCK
October 1996

Give honour unto Luke Evangelist:
  For he it was (the agèd legends say)
  Who first taught Art to fold her hands and pray. . . .

— Dante Gabriel Rossetti

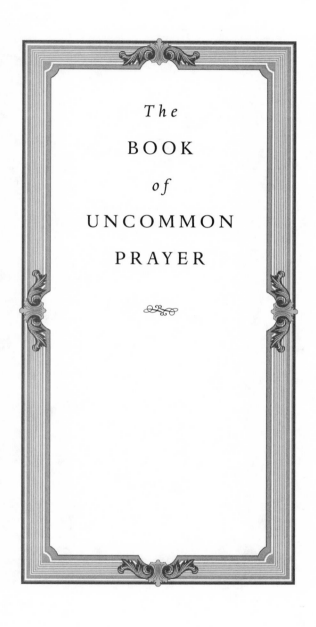

The

BOOK

of

UNCOMMON

PRAYER

My Little Kingdom

A little kingdom I possess,
    Where thoughts and feelings dwell,
And very hard I find the task
    Of governing it well;
For passion tempts and troubles me,
    A wayward will misleads,
And selfishness its shadow casts
    On all my words and deeds.

How can I learn to rule myself,
    To be the child I should,
Honest and brave, nor ever tire
    Of trying to be good?
How can I keep a sunny soul
    To shine along life's way?
How can I tune my little heart
    To sweetly sing all day?

Dear Father, help me with the love
    That casteth out my fear;
Teach me to lean on thee, and feel
    That thou art very near,
That no temptation is unseen,
    No childish grief too small,

Since thou, with patience infinite,
    Doth soothe and comfort all.

I do not ask for any crown
    But that which all may win,
Nor seek to conquer any world
    Except the one within.
Be thou my guide until I find,
    Led by a tender hand,
Thy happy kingdom in myself,
    And dare to take command.

Despondency

Silent and sad,
    When all are glad,
And the earth is dressed in flowers;
    When the gay birds sing
    Till the forests ring,
As they rest in woodland bowers.

    Oh, why these tears,
    And these idle fears
For what may come to-morrow?
    The birds find food
    From God so good,
And the flowers know no sorrow.

    If He clothes these
    And the leafy trees,

Will He not cherish thee?
  Why doubt His care;
  It is everywhere,
Though the way we may not see.

(poems written at the age of eleven)

Louisa May Alcott (1832–1888) was the American novelist and poet who wrote Little Women.

HENRY ADAMS

Help Me

Help me to see! not with my mimic sight —
   With yours! which carried radiance, like the sun,
Giving the rays you saw with — light in light —
   Tying all suns and stars and worlds in one.
Help me to know! not with my mocking art —
   With you, who know yourself unbound by laws;
Gave God your strength, your life, your sight, your
     heart,
   And took from him the Thought that Is— the
     Cause.
Help me to feel! not with my insect sense —
   With yours that felt all life alive in you;
Infinite heart beating at your expense;
   Infinite passion breathing the breath you drew!
Help me to bear! not my own baby load,
   But yours; who bore the failure of the light,
The strength, the knowledge and the thought of
     God—
   The futile folly of the Infinite!

    (from "Prayer to the Virgin of Chartres")

Henry Adams (1838–1918) was the
American historian and scholar who wrote
The Education of Henry Adams.

JANE AUSTEN

We Have Been Blessed Far Beyond

WE THANK THEE with all our hearts for every gracious dispensation, for all the blessings that have attended our lives, for every hour of safety, health, and peace, of domestic comfort and innocent enjoyment. We feel that we have been blessed far beyond any thing that we have deserved; and though we cannot but pray for a continuance of all these mercies, we acknowledge our unworthiness of them and implore thee to pardon the presumption of our desires.

Keep us oh! Heavenly Father from evil this night. Bring us in safety to the beginning of another day and grant that we may rise again with every serious and religious feeling which now directs us.

May thy mercy be extended over all mankind, bringing the ignorant to the knowledge of thy truth, awakening the impenitent, touching the hardened. Look with compassion upon the afflicted of every condition, assuage the pangs of disease, comfort the broken in spirit.

On Each Return of the Night

GIVE US GRACE, Almighty Father, so to pray, as to deserve to be heard, to address thee with our hearts, as with our lips. Thou art every where present, from thee no secret can be hid. May the knowledge of this teach us to fix our thoughts on thee, with reverence and devotion that we pray not in vain.

Look with mercy on the sins we have this day committed and in mercy make us feel them deeply, that our repentance may be sincere and our resolution steadfast of endeavouring against the commission of such in future. Teach us to understand the sinfulness of our own hearts, and bring to our knowledge every fault of temper and every evil habit in which we have indulged to the discomfort of our fellow-creatures, and the danger of our own souls.

May we now, and on each return of night, consider how the past day has been spent by us, what have been our prevailing thoughts, words, and actions during it, and how far we can acquit ourselves of evil. Have we thought irreverently of thee, have we disobeyed thy commandments, have we neglected any known duty, or willingly given pain to any human being? Incline us to ask our hearts these questions oh! God, and save us from deceiving ourselves by pride or vanity.

Give us a thankful sense of the blessings in which we live, of the many comforts of our lot; that we may not deserve to lose them by discontent or indifference. . . .

*Jane Austen (1775–1817) was the elegant
and witty British novelist who wrote*
Pride and Prejudice.

On Another's Sorrow

Can I see another's woe,
And not be in sorrow too?
Can I see another's grief,
And not seek for kind relief?

Can I see a falling tear,
And not feel my sorrow's share?
Can a father see his child
Weep, nor be with sorrow fill'd?

Can a mother sit and hear
An infant groan an infant fear?
No, no! never can it be!
Never, never can it be!

And can he who smiles on all
Hear the wren with sorrows small,
Hear the small bird's grief and care,
Hear the woes that infants bear,

And not sit beside the nest,
Pouring pity in their breast;
And not sit the cradle near,
Weeping tear on infant's tear;

And not sit both night and day,
Wiping all our tears away?

O, no! never can it be!
Never, never can it be!

He doth give his joy to all;
He becomes an infant small;
He becomes a man of woe;
He doth feel the sorrow too.

Think not thou canst sigh a sigh
And thy maker is not by;
Think not thou canst weep a tear
And thy maker is not near.

O! he gives to us his joy
That our grief he may destroy;
Till our grief is fled and gone
He doth sit by us and moan.

The Lamb

Little Lamb, who made thee?
    Dost thou know who made thee?
Gave thee life, and bid thee feed,
By the stream and o'er the mead;
Gave thee clothing of delight,
Softest clothing, woolly, bright;
Gave thee such a tender voice,
Making all the vales rejoice?
    Little Lamb, who made thee?
    Dost thou know who made thee?

Little Lamb, I'll tell thee,
Little Lamb, I'll tell thee:
He is callèd by thy name,
For He calls Himself a Lamb.
He is meek, and He is mild;
He became a little child.
I a child, and thou a lamb,
We are callèd by His name.
Little Lamb, God bless thee!
Little Lamb, God bless thee!

William Blake (1757–1827) was the visionary British artist and poet.

Ever Round His Throne

Oh! there lives within my heart
    A hope, long nursed by me;
(And should its cheering ray depart,
    How dark my soul would be!)

That as in Adam all have died,
    In Christ shall all men live;
And ever round His throne abide,
    Eternal praise to give.

That even the wicked shall at last
    Be fitted for the skies;
And when their dreadful doom is past,
    To life and light arise.

I ask not how remote the day,
    Nor what the sinners' woe,
Before their dross is purged away;
    Enough for me, to know

That when the cup of wrath is drained,
    The metal purified,
They'll cling to what they once disdained,
    And live by Him that died.

A Prayer

My God (oh, let me call Thee mine,
    Weak, wretched sinner though I be),
My trembling soul would fain be Thine;
    My feeble faith still clings to Thee.

Not only for the past I grieve,
    The future fills me with dismay;
Unless Thou hasten to relieve,
    Thy suppliant is a castaway.

I cannot say my faith is strong,
    I dare not hope my love is great;
But strength and love to Thee belong:
    Oh, do not leave me desolate!

I know I owe my all to Thee;
    Oh, take the heart I cannot give;
Do Thou my Strength, my Saviour be,
    And make me to Thy glory live!

Last Lines

A dreadful darkness closes in
    On my bewildered mind;
O let me suffer and not sin,
    Be tortured yet resigned.

Through all this world of blinding mist
    Still let me look to Thee,
And give me courage to resist
    The Tempter till he flee.

Weary I am, O give me strength
    And leave me not to faint;
Say Thou wilt comfort me at length
    And pity my complaint.

I've begged to serve Thee heart and soul,
    To sacrifice to Thee
No niggard portion, but the whole
    Of my identity . . .

O Thou hast taken my delight
    And hope of life away,
And bid me watch the painful night
    And wait the weary day.

The hope and the delight were Thine:
    I bless Thee for their loan;
I gave Thee while I deemed them mine
    Too little thanks I own.

Shall I with joy Thy blessings share
    And not endure their loss,
Or hope the martyr's Crown to wear
    And cast away the Cross?

*Anne Brontë (1820–1849), youngest of the three
Brontë sisters, wrote poems and hymns.*

CHARLOTTE BRONTË

On the Death of Anne Brontë

There's little joy in life for me,
    And little terror in the grave;
I've lived the parting hour to see
    Of one I would have died to save.

Calmly to watch the failing breath,
    Wishing each sigh might be the last;
Longing to see the shade of death
    O'er those beloved features cast.

The cloud, the stillness that must part
    The darling of my life from me;
And then to thank God from my heart,
    To thank Him well and fervently;

Although I knew that we had lost
    The hope and glory of our life;
And now, benighted, tempest-tossed,
    Must bear alone the weary strife.

On the Death of Emily Brontë

My darling, thou wilt never know
The grinding agony of woe
    That we have borne for thee.

Thus may we consolation tear
E'en from the depth of our despair
   And wasting misery.

The nightly anguish thou art spared
When all the crushing truth is bared
   To the awakening mind,
When the galled heart is pierced with grief,
Till wildly it implores relief,
   But small relief can find.

Nor know'st thou what it is to lie
Looking forth with streaming eye
   On life's lone wilderness.
"Weary, weary, dark and drear,
How shall I the journey bear,
   The burden and distress?"

Then since thou art spared such pain
We will not wish thee here again;
   He that lives must mourn.
God help us through our misery
And give us rest and joy with thee
   When we reach our bourne!

*Charlotte Brontë (1816–1855) was the British
novelist who wrote* Jane Eyre.

Last Lines

No coward soul is mine,
No trembler in the world's storm-troubled sphere;
    I see Heaven's glories shine,
And faith shines equal, arming me from fear.

    O God within my breast,
Almighty, ever-present Deity!
    Life — that in me has rest,
As I — undying life — have power in Thee!

    Vain are the thousand creeds
That move men's hearts: unutterably vain;
    Worthless as withered weeds,
Or idlest froth amid the boundless main.

    To waken doubt in one
Holding so fast by Thine infinity;
    So surely anchored on
The steadfast rock of immortality.

    With wide-embracing love
Thy Spirit animates eternal years,
    Pervades and broods above,
Changes, sustains, dissolves, creates, and rears.

    Though earth and man were gone,
And suns and universes ceased to be,
    And Thou were left alone,

Every existence would exist in Thee.

There is not room for Death
Nor atom that high might could render void:
Thou—THOU art Being and Breath,
And what THOU art may never be destroyed.

Courage

Riches I hold in light esteem
And Love I laugh to scorn
And lust of Fame was but a dream
That vanished with the morn—

And if I pray, the only prayer
That moves my lips for me
Is—"Leave the heart that now I bear
And give me liberty."

Yes, as my swift days near their goal
'Tis all that I implore—
Through life and death a chainless soul
With courage to endure!

Wanderer, Pray

The starry night shall tidings bring:
    Go out upon the breezy moor—
Watch for a bird with sable wing,
    And beak and talons dropping gore.

Look not around, look not beneath,
    But mutely trace its airy way—

Mark where it lights upon the heath;
   Then, wanderer, kneel thee down and pray.

What fortune may await thee there,
   I will not, and I dare not tell;
But Heaven is moved by fervent prayer,
   And God is mercy; fare thee well!

Emily Brontë (1818–1848) was the British novelist who wrote Wuthering Heights.

A Gauntlet, a Gift

God answers sharp and sudden on some prayers,
And thrusts the thing we have prayed for in our face,
A gauntlet with a gift in't.

My Days Go On

I praise Thee while my days go on;
I love Thee while my days go on:
Through dark and dearth, through fire and frost,
With emptied arms and treasure lost,
I thank Thee while my days go on.

Consolation

All are not taken; there are left behind
Living Beloveds, tender looks to bring
And make the daylight still a happy thing,
And tender voices, to make soft the wind:
But if it were not so—if I could find
No love in all the world for comforting,
Nor any path but hollowly did ring
Where "dust to dust" the love from life disjoined,
And if, before those sepulchers unmoving

I stood alone (as some forsaken lamb
Goes bleating up the moors in weary dearth)
Crying "Where are ye, O my loved and loving?"—
I know a Voice would sound, "Daughter, I AM.
Can I suffice for HEAVEN and not for earth?"

Holy Mysteries

God keeps His holy mysteries
    Just on the outside of man's dream;
In diapason slow, we think
To hear their pinions rise and sink,
While they float pure beneath His eyes,
    Like swans adown a stream.

Abstractions, are they, from the forms
    Of His great beauty?—exaltations
From His great glory?—strong previsions
Of what we shall be?—intuitions
Of what we are—in calms and storms
    Beyond our peace and passions?

Things nameless! which, in passing so,
    Do stroke us with a subtle grace;
We say, "Who passes?"—they are dumb;
We cannot see them go or come,
Their touches fall soft, cold, as snow
    Upon a blind man's face.

Yet, touching so they draw above
    Our common thoughts to Heaven's
unknown;

Our daily joy and pain advance
To a divine significance,
Our human love — O mortal love,
    That light is not its own!

*Elizabeth Barrett Browning (1806–1861) was
the delicate British poetess who wrote
Sonnets From the Portuguese.*

Song

The year's at the spring
And day's at the morn;
Morning's at seven;
The hillside's dew-pearled;
The lark's on the wing;
The snail's on the thorn;
God's in His heaven—
All's right with the world!

(from "Pippa Passes")

The Infinite Care

Have I knowledge? confounded it
    shrivels at Wisdom laid bare.
Have I forethought? how purblind,
    how blank, to the Infinite Care!
Do I task any faculty highest, to
    image success?
I but open my eyes—and perfection,
    no more and no less,
In the kind I imagined, full-fronts
    me, and God is seen God

In the star, in the stone, in the flesh,
    in the soul and the clod.
And thus looking within and around
    me, I ever renew
(With that stoop of the soul which
    in bending upraises it too)
The submission of man's nothing-
    perfect to God's all-complete,
As by each new obeisance in spirit, I
    climb to his feet.

He Guides Me

In some good time, his good time, I shall arrive:
He guides me and the bird. In his good time!

Robert Browning (1812–1889) was a
British Victorian poet.

WILLIAM CULLEN BRYANT

The Hour of Death

I would that thus, when I shall see
The hour of death draw near to me,
Hope, blossoming within my heart,
May look to heaven as I depart.

Pleasant Dreams

So live, that when thy summons comes to join
The innumerable caravan, which moves
To that mysterious realm, where each shall take
His chamber in the silent halls of death,
Thou go not, like the quarry-slave at night,
Scourged to his dungeon, but, sustained and soothed
By an unfaltering trust, approach thy grave
Like one who wraps the drapery of his couch
About him, and lies down to pleasant dreams.

(from "Thanatopsis")

*William Cullen Bryant (1794–1878) was an American
newspaper editor and poet of nature.*

THOMAS CARLYLE

❦

Do One

To shape the whole Future is not our problem; but only to shape faithfully a small part of it, according to rules already known. It is perhaps possible for each of us, who will with due earnestness inquire, to ascertain clearly what he, for his own part, ought to do; this let him, with true heart, do, and continue doing. The general issue will, as it has always done, rest well with a Higher Intelligence than ours. This day thou knowest ten commanded duties, seest in thy mind ten things which should be done for one that thou doest! *Do* one of them; this of itself will show thee ten others which can and shall be done.

Complain Not

Who art thou that complainest of thy life of toil? Complain not. Look up, my wearied brother; see thy fellow-workmen there, in God's Eternity; surviving there, they alone surviving; sacred band of the Immortals, celestial body-guard of the empire of mankind. To thee Heaven, though severe, is *not* unkind; Heaven is kind, as a noble mother; as that

Spartan mother, saying while she gave her son his shield, "With it, my son, or upon it." Thou too shalt return *home* in honor; to thy far-distant Home, in honor; doubt it not, if in the battle thou keep thy shield! Thou, in the Eternities and deepest death-kingdoms art not an alien; thou everywhere art a denizen. Complain not.

Thomas Carlyle (1795–1881) was a British historian, philosopher, and essayist.

GEOFFREY CHAUCER

Ballade of Good Counsel

Flee from the crowd and dwell with truthfulness:
  Suffice thee with thy goods, though they be
small:
To hoard brings hate, to climb brings giddiness;
  The crowd has envy, and success blinds all;
  Desire no more than to thy lot may fall;
Work well thyself to counsel others clear,
And Truth shall make thee free, there is no fear!

Torment thee not all crooked to redress,
  Nor put thy trust in fortune's turning ball;
Great peace is found in little busy-ness;
  And war but kicks against a sharpened awl;
  Strive not, thou earthen pot, to break the wall;
Subdue thyself, and others thee shall hear;
And Truth shall make thee free, there is no fear!

What God doth send, receive in gladsomeness;
  To wrestle for this world foretells a fall.
Here is no home, here is but wilderness:
  Forth, pilgrim, forth! Up, beast, and leave thy
stall!
  Know thy country, look up, thank God for all:
Hold the high way, thy soul the pioneer;
And Truth shall make thee free, there is no fear!

Therefore, poor beast, forsake thy wretchedness;
    No longer let the vain world be thy stall.
His mercy seek who in his mightiness
    Made thee of naught, but not to be a thrall.
    Pray freely for thyself and pray for all
Who long for larger life and heavenly cheer;
And Truth shall make thee free, there is no fear!

Be Our Guide

O Mother Maid! O Maid and Mother free!
O bush unburnt! burning in Moses' sight!
That down didst ravish from the Deity,
Through humbleness, the spirit that did alight
Upon thy heart, whence, through that glory's might,
Conceivèd was the Father's sapience,
Help me to tell it in thy reverence!

Lady! thy goodness, thy magnificence,
Thy virtue, and thy great humility,
Surpass all science and all utterance;
For sometimes, Lady! ere men pray to thee
Thou goest before in thy benignity,
The light to us vouchsafing of thy prayer,
To be our guide unto thy Son so dear.

My knowledge is so weak, O blissful Queen!
To tell abroad thy mighty worthiness,
That I the weight of it may not sustain;
But as a child of twelve months old or less,
That laboreth his language to express,

Even so fare I, and therefore, I thee pray,
Guide thou my song which I of thee shall say.

(from "The Prioress' Tale")

*Geoffrey Chaucer (1340–1400) was the British poet
who wrote* The Canterbury Tales.

SAMUEL TAYLOR COLERIDGE

Prayeth, Loveth

He prayeth well who loveth well
  Both man and bird and beast;
He prayeth best who loveth best
  All things both great and small;
For the dear God who loveth us,
  He made and loveth all.

*Samuel Taylor Coleridge (1772–1834) was the
British poet, critic, and philosopher who wrote*
The Rime of the Ancient Mariner.

DANIEL DEFOE

❦

Give Me Repentance

JULY 4. In the morning I took the Bible, and beginning at the New Testament, I began seriously to read it, and impos'd upon myself to read a while every morning and every night, not tying myself to the number of chapters, but as long as my thoughts should engage me. It was not long after I set seriously to this work, but I found my heart more deeply and sincerely affected with the wickedness of my past life. The impression of my dream revived, and the words, "All these things have not brought thee to repentance," ran seriously in my thought. I was earnestly begging of God to give me repentance, when it happened providentially the very day that, reading the Scripture, I came to these words, "He is exalted a Prince and a Saviour, to give repentance, and to give remission." I threw down the book, and with my heart as well as my hands lifted up to Heaven, in a kind of ecstasy of joy, I cried out aloud, "Jesus, thou son of David, Jesu, thou exalted Prince and Saviour, give me repentance!"

This was the first time that I could say, in the true sense of the words, that I prayed in all my life; for now I prayed with a sense of my condition, and with a true Scripture view of hope founded on the encouragement

of the Word of God; and from this time, I may say, I
began to have hope that God would hear me.

(from *Robinson Crusoe*)

*Daniel Defoe (1660–1731) was the British
author of* The Life and Strange Surprizing
Adventures of Robinson Crusoe.

CHARLES DICKENS

❧

No Other Commandment Greater

HEAR WHAT our Lord Jesus Christ taught to His
Disciples and to us, and what we should remember every day of our lives, to love the Lord our God with
all our heart, and with all our mind, and with all our
soul, and with all our strength; to love our neighbours as
ourselves, to do unto other people as we would have
them do unto us and to be charitable and gentle to all.

There is no other commandment, our Lord Jesus
Christ said, greater than these. Amen.

For the Evening

O GOD, who has made everything, and is so kind
and merciful to everything He has made that tries
to be good and to deserve it; God bless my dear Papa
and Mama, Brothers and Sisters and all my Relations
and Friends. Make me a good little child, and let me
never be naughty and tell a lie, which is a mean and
shameful thing. Make me kind to all beggars and poor
people, and let me never be cruel to any dumb creatures, for if I am cruel to anything, even to a poor little
fly, God, who is so good, will never love me. And pray

God to bless and preserve us all, this night, and forever-
more, through Jesus Christ our Lord. Amen.

(written for his young children)

*Charles Dickens (1812–1870) was the beloved British
novelist who wrote* David Copperfield.

EMILY DICKINSON

In God's Ear

Prayer is the little implement
Through which men reach
where Presence is denied them.
They fling their speech

By means of it in God's Ear
If then He hear.
This sums the apparatus
Comprised in prayer.

Chartless

I never saw a moor,
I never saw the sea;
Yet know I how the heather looks,
And what a wave must be.

I never spoke with God,
Nor visited in heaven;
Yet certain am I of the spot
As if the chart were given.

Your Soul

He fumbles at your soul
As players at the keys
Before they drop full music on,
He stuns you by degrees,
Prepares your brittle nature
For the ethereal blow
By fainter hammers, further heard,
Then nearer—then so slow
Your breath has time to straighten,
Your brain to bubble cool—
Deals one imperial thunderbolt
That scalps your naked soul.

This World

This world is not conclusion;
    A sequel stands beyond,
Invisible, as music,
    But positive, as sound.
It beckons and it baffles;
    Philosophies don't know,
And through a riddle, at the last,
    Sagacity must go.
To guess it puzzles scholars;
    To gain it, men have shown
Contempt of generations,
    And crucifixion known.

Going to Heaven!

Going to Heaven!
I don't know when —
Pray do not ask me how!
Indeed I'm too astonished
To think of answering you!
Going to Heaven!
How dim it sounds!
And yet it will be done
As sure as flocks go home at night
Unto the Shepherd's arm!

Perhaps you're going too!
Who knows?
If you should get there first
Save just a little space for me
Close to the two I lost —
The smallest "Robe" will fit me
And just a bit of "Crown" —
For you know we do not mind our dress
When we are going home —

*Emily Dickinson (1830–1886) was the brilliant,
enigmatic American poetess.*

JOHN DONNE

Epiphany

THE WHOLE life of Christ was a continual Passion; others die martyrs but Christ was born a martyr. He found a Golgotha even in Bethlehem, where he was born; for to his tenderness then the straws were almost as sharp as the thorns after, and the manger as uneasy at first as his cross at last. His birth and his death were but one continual act, and his Christmas Day and his Good Friday are but the evening and morning of one and the same day. And as even his birth is his death, so every action and passage that manifests Christ to us is his birth, for *Epiphany is manifestation.*

A Plea for Mercy

O LORD, I most humbly acknowledge and confess that I have understood sin, by understanding thy laws and judgments; but have gone against thy known and revealed will. Thou hast set up many candlesticks, and kindled many lamps in me; but I have either blown them out, or carried them to guide me in forbidden ways. Thou hast given me a desire of knowledge, and some means to it, and some possession of it; and I have armed myself with thy weapons against thee. Yet, O God, have mercy upon me, for thine own sake have mercy upon me. Let not sin and me be able to exceed thee, nor to defraud thee, nor to frustrate thy purposes. But let me, in spite of me, be of so much use to thy glory, that by thy mercy to my sin, other sinners may see how much sin thou canst pardon.

Preserve My Soul

ETERNAL and most glorious God, suffer me not so to undervalue myself as to give away my soul, Thy soul, Thy dear and precious soul, for nothing; and all the world is nothing, if the soul must be given for it. Preserve therefore, my soul, O Lord, because it belongs to Thee, and preserve my body because it belongs to my soul. Thou alone dost steer my boat through all its voyage, but hast a more especial care of it, when it comes to a narrow current, or to a dangerous fall of waters. Thou hast a care of the preservation of my body in all the ways of my life; but, in the straits of death, open Thine eyes wider, and enlarge Thy Providence toward me so far that no illness or agony may shake and benumb the soul. Do Thou so make my bed in all my sickness that, being used to Thy hand, I may be content with any bed of Thy making.

A Hymn to God the Father

Wilt Thou forgive that sin where I begun;
    Which was my sin, though it were done before?
Wilt Thou forgive that sin through which I run,
    And do run still, though still I do deplore?
When Thou hast done, Thou hast not done;
      For I have more.
Wilt Thou forgive that sin which I have won
    Others to sin, and made my sins their door?
Wilt Thou forgive that sin which I did shun
    A year or two, but wallowed in a score?
When Thou hast done, Thou hast not done;
      For I have more.
I have a sin of fear, that when I've spun
    My last thread, I shall perish on the shore;
But swear by Thyself that at my death Thy Son
    Shall shine as He shines now, and heretofore;
And having done that, Thou hast done,
      I fear no more.

A Vision of Heaven

Bring us, O Lord God, at the last awakening into the house and gate of heaven, to enter into that gate and dwell in that house, where there shall be no darkness nor dazzling, but one equal light; no noise nor silence, but one equal music; no fears nor hopes, but an equal possession; no ends nor beginnings, but one equal eternity, in the habitations of thy majesty and thy glory, world without end.

John Donne (1572–1631) was the metaphysical British poet and preacher.

FYODOR DOSTOYEVSKY

Have Mercy on Those Who Come Before Thee

EACH TIME you pray, if your prayer is sincere, there will be new feeling in it, and a new meaning, which will give you fresh courage; and you will understand that prayer is an education. Remember also, every day and whenever you can, repeat to yourself, "Lord, have mercy on all who come before Thee today." For every hour and every moment thousands of people leave their life on this earth, and their souls appear before God. And so many of them depart alone, unknown, in sadness and sorrow that no one will mourn them, or even know whether they had lived or not. And so, perhaps from the other end of the earth, your prayer for their repose will rise up to God, though you did not know them, nor they you. How touching it must be to a soul, coming in fear before the Lord, to feel at that moment that someone is praying for him, too, that there is still a fellow creature on earth who loves him. And God will look upon you both with more mercy, for if you have so pitied him, how much more will He who is infinitely more merciful and loving than you. And He will forgive him for your sake.

I Love Thee

L ORD, have mercy on me, with all my lawlessness. Let me pass by Thy judgment. Do not judge me, for I have condemned myself, do not condemn me, for I love Thee, O Lord. I am a wretch, but I love Thee. If Thou sendest me to hell, even there I shall love Thee, and from there I shall cry out that I love Thee forever and ever.

(from *The Brothers Karamazov*)

Fyodor Dostoyevsky (1821–1881) was the Russian novelist and journalist who wrote Crime and Punishment *and* The Brothers Karamazov.

JOHN DRYDEN

Mysterious Things of Faith

Can I believe eternal God could lie
Disguised in mortal mould and infancy?
That the great Maker of the world could die?
And after that trust my imperfect sense,
Which calls in question his omnipotence?
Can I reason to my faith compel,
And shall my sight, and touch, and taste rebel?
Superior faculties are set aside;
Shall their subservient organs be my guide?
Then let the moon usurp the role of day,
And winking tapers show the sun his way;
For what my senses can themselves perceive,
I need no revelation to believe . . .
To prove the Godhead of the eternal Son,
God thus asserted: man is to believe
Beyond what sense and reason can conceive,
And for mysterious things of faith rely
On the proponent, Heaven's authority.
If then our faith we for our guide admit,
Vain is the farther search of human wit;
As, when the building gains a surer stay,
We take the unuseful scaffolding away . . .

Veni, Creator Spiritus

Creator Spirit, by whose aid
The world's foundations first were laid,
Come visit every pious mind;
Come pour thy joys on humankind;
From sin and sorrow set us free,
And make thy temples worthy thee . . .
Refine and purge our earthy parts;
But, O, inflame and fire our hearts!
Our frailties help, our vice control,
Submit the senses to the soul;
And when rebellious they are grown,
Then lay thy hand and hold them down.
Chase from our minds the infernal foe,
And peace, the fruit of love, bestow;
And lest our feet should step astray,
Protect and guide us in the way.
Make us eternal truths receive,
And practice all that we believe;
Give us thyself that we may see
The Father and the Son, by thee.

Guide Us Upward

Dim as the borrowed beams of moon and stars
To lonely, weary, wandering travelers,
Is reason to the soul; and as on high,
Those rolling fires discover but the sky,
Not light us here; so Reason's glimmering ray
Was lent, not to assure us of our doubtful way,

But guide us upward to a better day.
And as those nightly tapers disappear,
When day's bright lord ascends our hemisphere;
So pale grows Reason at Religion's sight;
So dies, and so dissolves in supernatural light.

*John Dryden (1631–1700) was a British poet,
dramatist, and critic.*

GEORGE ELIOT

❧

At His Feet

As soon as we lay ourselves entirely at His feet, we have enough light given us to guide our own steps; as the foot-soldier, who hears nothing of the councils that determine the course of the great battle he is in, hears plainly enough the word of command which he must himself obey.

A River

You are seeking your own will . . . You are seeking some good other than the law you are bound to obey. But how will you find good? It is not a thing of choice; it is a river that flows from the foot of the Invisible Throne, and flows by the path of obedience. I say again, man cannot choose his duties. You may choose to forsake your duties, and choose not to have the sorrow they bring. But you will go forth, and what will you find? Sorrow without duty—bitter herbs, and no bread with them.

George Eliot (1819–1880) was the pen name of Mary Ann Evans, the British novelist who wrote Silas Marner.

RALPH WALDO EMERSON

On Our Faces

THE GODS we worship write their names on our
faces, be sure of that. And a man will worship
something —have no doubt about that, either. He may
think that his tribute is paid in secret in the dark recess-
es of his heart—but it will out. That which dominates
will determine his life and character. Therefore, it
behooves us to be careful what we worship, for what we
are worshipping we are becoming.

We Thank Thee

For flowers that bloom about our feet;
For tender grass, so fresh and sweet;
For song of bird and hum of bee;
For all things fair we hear or see
Father in Heaven, we thank Thee!

For blue of stream, for blue of sky;
For pleasant shade of branches high;
For fragrant air and cooling breeze;
For beauty of the blowing trees—
Father in Heaven, we thank Thee!

For mother-love, for father-care;
For brothers strong and sisters fair;
For love at home and school each day;
for guidance lest we go astray—
Father in Heaven, we thank Thee!

For Thy dear, everlasting arms,
That bear us o'er all ills and harms;
For blessed words of long ago,
That help us now Thy will to know—
Father in Heaven, we thank Thee!

Row Away

Call on God, but row away from the rocks.

The Heart of Love

April cold with dropping rain
Willows and lilacs brings again,
The whistle of returning birds,
And the trumpet-lowing of the herds.
The scarlet maple-keys betray
What potent blood hath modest May,
What fiery force the earth renews,
The wealth of forms, the flush of hues;
What joy in rosy waves outpoured
Flows from the heart of Love, the Lord.

Listen to the Soul

T HAT WHICH befits us, embosomed in beauty and wonder as we are, is cheerfulness, and courage, and the endeavor to realize our aspirations. Shall not the heart which has received so much, trust the Power by which it lives? May it not quit other leadings, and listen to the Soul that has guided it so gently, and taught it so much, secure that the future will be worthy of the past?

Ralph Waldo Emerson (1803–1882) was the Transcendentalist American philosopher, poet, and essayist.

DESIDERIUS ERASMUS

❧

The True Sun

Thou, who art the true Sun of the world, evermore rising, and never going down; who, by Thy most wholesome appearing and sight dost nourish, and make joyful all things as well that are in heaven, as also that are on earth; we beseech Thee mercifully and favorably to shine into our hearts, that the night and darkness of sin, and the mists of error on every side, being driven away, Thou brightly shining within our hearts, we may all our life long go without any stumbling or offence, and may walk as in the day-time, being pure and clean from the works of darkness, and abounding in all good works which Thou hast prepared for us to walk in.

Thy Holy Breath

O Holy Spirit, which with thy holy breath cleans men's minds, comforting them when they be in sorrow, cheering them up with pure gladness, when they be in heaviness, leading them into all truth, when they be out of the way, kindling in them the fire of charity, when they be cold, knitting them together with the glue of peace, when they be at variance, and garnishing and enriching them with sundry gifts, which by thy means profess the name of the Lord Jesus: by whose working all things live, which live in deed: whose delight is to dwell in the hearts of the simple, which thou hast vouchsafed to consecrate for temples, to thyself.

I beseech thee, maintain thy gifts in me, and increase the things daily, which thou hast vouchsafed to bestow upon me, that by thy governance the lusts of the flesh may die more and more in me and the desire of the heavenly life more quicken and increase.

Let me so pass through the misty desert of this world by thy light going before me; as I may neither be defiled with Satan's wiles, nor be entangled with any errors disagreeing from thy truth.

Abound in You

Sever me from myself that I may be grateful to you;
may I perish to myself that I may be safe in you;
may I die to myself that I may live in you;
may I wither to myself that I may blossom in you;
may I be emptied of myself that I may abound in you;
may I be nothing to myself that I may be all to you.

Desiderius Erasmus (1466–1536) was a
Dutch theologian and scholar.

The Light of Eternal Love

And I press on with a lighter heart
Through all the ways of the endless rings.
The pure word of the living God
Moves in the depths of them and sings.

Unhampered now by fierce desire
We follow and find no ending here
Till in the light of eternal Love
We melt, we disappear.

Above Earthly Control

No PRODUCTIVENESS of the highest kind, no remarkable discovery, no great thought that bears fruit and has results, is in the power of anyone; such things are above earthly control. Man must consider them as an unexpected gift from above, as pure children of God which he must receive and venerate with joyful thanks.

(from *Conversations with Eckermann*)

Chorus of Angels

Christ is arisen,
Out of corruption's womb:
Burst ye the prison,
Break from your gloom!
Praising and pleading him,
Lovingly needing him,
Brotherly feeding him,
Preaching and speeding him,
Blessing, succeeding Him,
Thus is the Master near,
Thus is He here!

(from *Faust*)

Johann Wolfgang von Goethe (1749–1832) was the German poet, novelist, essayist, and dramatist who wrote Faust.

Quick-Eyed Love

Love bade me welcome; yet my soul drew back,
  Guilty of dust and sin.
But quick-eyed Love, observing me grow slack
  From my first entrance in,
Drew nearer to me, sweetly questioning
  If I lack'd anything.

"A guest," I answer'd, "worthy to be here:"
  Love said, "You shall be he."
"I, the unkind, ungrateful? Ah, my dear,
  I cannot look on Thee."
Love took my hand and smiling did reply,
  "Who made the eyes but I?"

"Truth, Lord, but I have marr'd them: let my shame
  Go where it doth deserve."
"And know you not," says Love, "Who bore the
  blame?"
  "My dear, then I will serve."
"You must sit down," says Love, "and taste my meat."
  So I did set and eat.

The Altar

A broken altar, Lord, thy servant rears,
Made of a heart and cemented with tears;
  Whose parts are as thy hand did frame;
  No workman's tool hath touched the same.

                A   heart   alone
                Is   such   a   stone
                As   nothing   but
                Thy power doth cut.
                Wherefore each part
                Of my hard heart
                Meets in this frame
                To praise thy name;

  That if I chance to hold my peace,
These stones to praise thee may not cease.
Oh, let thy blessed sacrifice be mine,
And sanctify this altar to be thine.

George Herbert (1593–1633) was an
English poet and clergyman.

ROBERT HERRICK

A Grace

Here, a little child, I stand,
Heaving up my either hand;
Cold as paddocks though they be,
Here I lift them up to thee,
For a benison to fall
On our meat and on our all.

His Litany to the Holy Spirit

In the hour of my distress,
When temptations me oppress,
And when I my sins confess,
    Sweet Spirit comfort me!

When I lie within my bed,
Sick in heart and sick in head,
And with doubts discomforted,
    Sweet Spirit comfort me!

When the house doth sigh and weep,
And the world is drowned in sleep,
Yet mine eyes the watch do keep,
    Sweet Spirit comfort me!

When the artless Doctor sees
No one hope but of his fees,
And his skill runs on the lees,
   Sweet Spirit comfort me!

When his potion and his pill,
His, or none, or little skill,
Meets for nothing but to kill,
   Sweet Spirit comfort me!

When the passing-bell doth toll,
And the Furies in a shoal,
Come to fright a parting soul,
   Sweet Spirit comfort me!

When the tapers burn blue,
And the comforters are few,
And that number more than true,
   Sweet Spirit comfort me!

When the priest his last hath prayed,
And I nod to what is said,
'Cause my speech is now decayed,
   Sweet Spirit comfort me!

When (God knows) I'm tossed about,
Either with despair or doubt,
Yet before the glass be out,
   Sweet Spirit comfort me!

When the Tempter me pursu'th
With the sins of all my youth,
And half damns me with untruth,
   Sweet Spirit comfort me!

When the flames and hellish cries
Fright mine ears and fright mine eyes,

And all terrors me surprise,
  Sweet Spirit comfort me!

When the judgment is revealed,
And that opened which was sealed,
When to thee I have appealed,
  Sweet Spirit comfort me!

*Robert Herrick (1591–1674) was the
British Cavalier poet.*

OLIVER WENDELL HOLMES

The Outgrown Shell

Build thee more stately mansions, O my soul,
　　As the swift seasons roll!
　　Leave thy low-vaulted past!
Let each new temple, nobler than the last,
Shut thee from heaven with a dome more vast,
　　Till thou at length art free,
Leaving thine outgrown shell by life's unresting sea!

(from *The Nautilus*)

*Oliver Wendell Holmes (1809–1894) was an
American writer and physician—and father
of the Supreme Court justice.*

O God, I Love Thee

O God, I love thee, I love thee—
Not out of hope of heaven for me
Nor fearing not to love and be
   In the everlasting burning.
Thou, thou, my Jesus, after me
   Didst reach thine arms out dying,
For my sake sufferedst nails and lance,
Mocked and marrèd countenance,
   Sorrows passing number,
   Sweat and care and cumber,
Yea and death, and this for me,
   And thou couldst see me sinning:
Then I, why should not I love thee,
Jesu so much in love with me?
Not for heaven's sake; not to be
Out of hell by loving thee;
Not for any gains I see;
But just the way that thou didst me
I do love and I will love thee:
What must I love thee, Lord, for then?—
For being my king and God. Amen.

Thou Art Indeed Just, Lord

Thou art indeed just, Lord, if I contend
With thee; but, sir, so what I plead is just.
Why do sinners' ways prosper? And why must
Disappointment all I endeavor end?

Wert thou my enemy, O thou my friend,
How wouldst thou worse, I wonder, than thou dost
Defeat, thwart me? Oh, the sots and thralls of lust
Do in spare hours more thrive than I that spend,
Sir, life upon thy cause. See, banks and brakes
Now, leavèd how thick! lacèd they are again
With fretty chervil, look, and fresh wind shakes

Them; birds build—but not I build; no, but strain,
Time's eunuch, and not breed one work that wakes.
Mine, O thou lord of life, send my roots rain.

Godhead in Hiding

Godhead here in hiding, whom I do adore
Masked by these bare shadows, shape
    and nothing more,
See, Lord, at thy service low lies here a heart
Lost, all lost in wonder at the God thou art . . .

Jesu whom I look at shrouded here below,
I beseech thee send me what I thirst for so,
Some day to gaze on thee face to face in light
And be blest for ever with thy glory's sight.

Pied Beauty

Glory be to God for dappled things —
  For skies of couple-color as a brindled cow;
  For rose-moles all in stipple upon trout that
swim;
Fresh-firecoal chestnut falls; finches' wings;
  Landscape plotted and pieced-fold, fallow, and
plough;
  And all trades, their gear and tackle and trim.

All things counter, original, spare, strange;
  Whatever is fickle, freckled (who knows how?)
  With swift, slow; sweet, sour; adazzle, dim;
He fathers-forth whose beauty is past change;
    Praise him.

*Gerard Manley Hopkins (1844–1889) was the
British priest and mystic-poet.*

VICTOR HUGO

The Soul

CERTAIN THOUGHTS are prayers. There are moments when, whatever be the attitude of the body, the soul is on its knees.

Life Uncertain

What matter it though life uncertain be
    To all? What though its goal
Be never reached? What though it fall and flee—
    Have we not each a soul?
Be like the bird that on a bough too frail
    To bear him gaily swings;
He carols though the slender branches fail—
    He knows he has wings!

Grief

GRIEF IS a fruit; God does not make it grow upon a branch too feeble to bear it.

Victor Hugo (1802–1885) was the French poet, dramatist, and novelist who wrote Les Miserables.

HELEN HUNT JACKSON

A Last Prayer

Father, I scarcely dare to pray,
    So clear I see, now it is done,
That I have wasted half my day
    And left my work but just begun.

So clear I see that things I thought
    Were right, or harmless, were a sin;
So clear I see that I have sought
    Unconscious, selfish aims to win;

So clear I see that I have hurt
    The souls I might have helped to save;
That I have slothful been, inert,
    Deaf to the calls Thy leaders gave.

In outskirts of thy kingdom vast,
    Father, the humblest spot give me;
Set me the lowliest task thou hast;
    Let me, repentant, work for thee.

*Helen Hunt Jackson (1830–1885) was the American
poet and novelist who wrote* Ramona.

SAMUEL JOHNSON

Made Perfect Through Suffering

I bless thee, Lord, for sorrows sent
　　To break my dream of human power;
For now, my shallow cistern spent,
　　I find thy founts, and thirst no more.

I take Thy hand, and fears grow still;
　　Behold thy face, and doubts remove;
Who would not yield his wavering will
　　To perfect Truth and boundless Love?

That Love this restless soul doth teach
　　The strength of thine eternal calm;
And tune its sad but broken speech
　　To join on earth the angel's psalm.

Oh, be it patient in thy hands,
　　And drawn, through each mysterious hour,
To service of thy pure commands,
　　The narrow way of Love and Power.

Much to Be Done

O LORD, my maker and protector, who hast gra-
ciously sent me into this world, to work out my
salvation, enable me to drive from me all such unquiet

and perplexing thoughts as may mislead or hinder me in the practice of those duties which thou hast required. When I behold the works of thy hands and consider the course of thy providence, give me grace always to remember that thy thoughts are not my thoughts, nor thy ways my ways.

And while it shall please thee to continue me in this world where much is to be done and little to be known, teach me by thy Holy Spirit to withdraw my mind from unprofitable and dangerous enquiries, from difficulties vainly curious and doubts impossible to be solved. Let me rejoice in the light which thou hast imparted, let me serve thee with active zeal and humble confidence, and wait with patient expectation for the time in which the soul which thou receivest shall be satisfied with knowledge.

For Divine Strength

Father, in thy mysterious presence kneeling,
    Fain would our souls feel all thy kindling love;
For we are weak and need some deep revealing
    Of trust, and strength, and calmness from above.

Lord, we have wandered far through doubt and sorrow,
    And thou hast made each step an onward one;
And we will ever trust each unknown morrow—
    Thou wilt sustain us till its work is done.

In the heart's depth a peace serene and holy
    Abides; and when pain seems to have its will,
Or we despair, O may that peace rise slowly
    Stronger than agony, and we be still!

Studying Religion

ALMIGHTY GOD, our heavenly Father, without whose help labor is useless, without whose light search is vain, invigorate my studies and direct my enquiries, that I may, by due diligence and right discernment, establish myself and others in thy holy faith. Take not, O Lord, thy Holy Spirit from me; let not evil thoughts have domination in my mind. Let me not linger in ignorance, but enlighten and support me.

Samuel Johnson (1709–1784) was the British critic, poet, novelist, and lexicographer.

A Hymn to God the Father

Hear me, O God!
    A broken heart
    Is my best part:
Use still thy rod,
That I may prove,
    Therein, Thy love.

If Thou hadst not
    Been stern to me,
    But left me free,
I had forgot
    Myself and Thee.

For, sin's so sweet,
    As minds ill-bent
    Rarely repent,
Unless they meet
    Their punishment.

Who more can crave
    Than Thou hast done?
    Thou gavest a Son
To free a slave,
    First made of nought,
    With all since bought.

Sin, death, and hell
    His glorious Name
    Quite overcame;
Yet I rebel,
    And slight the same.

But, I'll come in
    Before my loss
    Me farther toss;
As sure to win
    Under His cross.

To Heaven

Good and great God, can I not think of thee
    But it must, straight, my melancholy be?
Is it interpreted in my disease
    That, laden with my sins, I seek for ease?
O be thou witness, that the reins dost know
    And hearts of all, if I be sad for show,
And judge me after, if I dare pretend
    To aught but grace, or aim at other end.
As thou art all, so be thou all to me,
    First, midst, and last, converted, one and three;
My faith, my hope, my love; and in this state
    My judge, my witness, and my advocate.
Where have I been this while exiled from thee,
    And whither rap'd, now thou but stoop'st to
me?
Dwell, dwell here still, O being everywhere,
    How can I doubt to find thee ever, here?

I know my state, both full of shame and scorn
　　Conceived in sin, and unto labor born,
Standing with fear, and must with horror fall,
　　And destined unto judgment, after all.
I feel my griefs, too, and there scarce is ground
　　Upon my flesh to inflict another wound.
Yet dare I not complain, or wish for death
　　With holy Paul, lest it be thought the breath
Of discontent; or that these prayers be
　　For weariness of life, not love of thee.

*Ben Jonson (1573–1637) was the British poet and
dramatist who wrote* Volpone.

Patience

YOU SUFFERED throughout your life, O Lord Jesus Christ, that I might be saved. And yet, even now, you continue to bear with me, as I stumble upon the path and constantly go astray. As often as I become impatient and wish to abandon your way, you encourage me and stretch forth your helping hand. Each day I increase your burden; yet while I am impatient, your patience is infinite.

Prayer

Prayer does not change God,
but it changes him who prays.

Under Your Wings

THE FOXES have holes, the birds of the air have nests, but you had nowhere to lay your head, O Lord. And yet you were a hiding place where the sinner could flee. Today you are still such a hiding place, and I flee to you. I hide myself under your wings, and your wings cover the multitude of my sins.

Your Hand, Lord Jesus

WE RECEIVE everything from your hand, Lord Jesus. Your powerful hand stretches forth and turns wordly wisdom into holy folly. Your gentle hand opens and offers the gift of inner peace. If ever it seems that your reach is shortened, it is only to increase our faith and trust, that we may reach out to you. And if ever it seems that your hand is withheld from us, we know that it is only to conceal the eternal blessing you have promised — that we may yearn for that blessing even more fervently.

You Redeem Us

TRIVIAL PLEASURES, unsatisfying pursuits, worthless cares — all these drag us back, O Lord. Pride that makes us loath to accept help, cowardice that flinches from sharing your suffering, anguish at the prospect of confessing our sins to you — all these frighten us away. Yet you are stronger than all these forces. You redeem us from our empty, trivial existence, you save us from our foolish fears. This is your labor which you have accomplished and continue to accomplish each moment.

Faith

TEACH ME, O God, not to torture myself, not to make a martyr out of myself through stifling reflection, but rather teach me to breathe deeply in faith.

Søren Kierkegaard (1813–1855) was the Danish philosopher who inspired the existentialists.

Trees

I think that I shall never see
A poem lovely as a tree.
A tree whose hungry mouth is prest
Against the earth's sweet flowing breast;
A tree that looks at God all day,
And lifts her leafy arms to pray;
A tree that may in Summer wear
A nest of robins in her hair;
Upon whose bosom snow has lain;
Who intimately lives with rain.
Poems are made by fools like me,
But only God can make a tree.

Prayer of a Soldier in France

My shoulders ache beneath the pack
(Lie easier, Cross, upon His back.)
I march with feet that burn and smart
(Tread, Holy Feet, upon my heart.)
Men shout at me who may not speak
(They scourged Thy back and smote Thy cheek.)
I may not lift a hand to clear

My eyes of salty drops that sear.
(Then shall my fickle soul forget
Thy Agony of Bloody Sweat?)
My rifle hand is stiff and numb
(From Thy pierced palm red rivers come.)
Lord, Thou didst suffer more for me
Than all the hosts of land and sea.
So, let me render back again
This millionth of Thy gift. Amen.

Joyce Kilmer (1886–1918) was an American poet and journalist who died on the battlefield in World War I.

RUDYARD KIPLING

The Glory of the Garden

Then seek your job with thankfulness and work
   till further orders,
If it's only netting strawberries or killing slugs
   on borders;
And when your back stops aching and your
   hands begin to harden,
You will find yourself a partner in the Glory of
   the Garden.
Oh, Adam was a gardener, and God who made
   him sees
That half a proper gardener's work is done upon
   his knees,
So when your work is finished, you can wash
   your hands and pray
For the Glory of the Garden, that it may not pass
   away!
And the Glory of the Garden it shall never pass away!

A Pilgrim's Way

Deliver me from every pride—the Middle, High,
    and Low—
That bars me from a brother's side, whatever
    pride he show.
And purge me from all heresies of thought and
    speech and pen
That bid me judge him otherwise than I am
    judged. *Amen*!

Teach Us

Father in Heaven who lovest all,
O help Thy children when they call;
That they may build from age to age
An undefiled heritage.

Teach us to rule ourselves alway,
Controlled and cleanly night and day;
That we may bring, if need arise,
No maimed or worthless sacrifice.

Teach us the strength that cannot seek,
By deed or thought, to hurt the weak:
That, under Thee, we may possess
Man's strength to comfort man's distress.

Teach us delight in simple things,
And mirth that has no bitter springs;
Forgiveness free of evil done,
And Love to all men 'neath the sun!

When Earth's Last Picture Is Painted

When Earth's last picture is painted and the
　　tubes are twisted and dried,
When the oldest colors have faded, and the
　　youngest critic has died,
We shall rest, and, faith, we shall need it—lie
　　down for an aeon or two,
Till the Master of All Good Workmen shall put
　　us to work anew!

And those that were good shall be happy: they
　　shall sit in a golden chair;
They shall splash at a ten-league canvas with
　　brushes of comets' hair.
They shall find real saints to draw
　　from—Magdalene, Peter, and Paul;
They shall work for an age at a sitting and never
　　be tired at all!

And only The Master shall praise us, and only
　　The Master shall blame;
And no one shall work for money, and no one
　　shall work for fame,
But each for the joy of the working, and each, in
　　his separate star,
Shall draw the Thing as he sees It for the God of
　　Things as They Are!

*Rudyard Kipling (1865–1936) was the British poet,
short-story writer, and novelist who wrote* Kim.

CHARLES LAMB

A Need for Grace

I OWN THAT I am disposed to say grace upon twenty other occasions in the course of the day besides my dinner. I want a form for setting out upon a pleasant walk, for a moonlight ramble, for a friendly meeting, or a solved problem. Why have we none for books, those spiritual repasts—a grace before Milton—a grace before Shakespeare—a devotional exercise proper to be said before reading *The Faerie Queene*?

Charles Lamb (1775–1834) was a British essayist, editor, and critic.

You May Say

YOU CAN SAY that Christ died for our sins. You may say that the Father has forgiven us because Christ has done for us what we ought to have done. You may say that we are washed in the blood of the Lamb. You may say that Christ has defeated death. They are all true. If any of them do not appeal to you, leave it alone and get on with the formula that does. And, whatever you do, do not start quarreling with other people because they use a different formula from yours.

God Shows Himself

PRAYER in the sense of petition, asking for things, is a small part of it; confession and penitence are its threshold, adoration its sanctuary, the presence and vision and enjoyment of God its bread and wine. In it God shows himself to us. That He answers prayers is a corollary—not necessarily the most important one—from that revelation. What He does is learned from what He is.

Supposing We Found Him?

THERE COMES a moment when people who have been dabbling in religion ("man's search for God") suddenly draw back. Supposing we really found Him? We never meant it to come to that! Worse still, supposing He had found us?

The Apologist's Evening Prayer

From all my lame defeats and oh! much more
From all the victories that I seemed to score;
From cleverness shot forth on Thy behalf
At which, while angels weep, the audience laugh;
From all my proofs of Thy divinity
Thou, who wouldst give no sign, deliver me.

Thoughts are but coins. Let me not trust, instead
Of Thee, their thin-worn image of Thy head.
From all my thoughts, even from my thoughts
    of Thee,
O thou fair Silence, fall, and set me free.
Lord of the narrow gate and the needle's eye,
Take from me all my trumpery lest I die.

C. S. Lewis (1898 – 1963) was the British writer noted for his eloquent advocacy of Christianity.

HERMAN MELVILLE

I Called My God

The ribs and terrors in the whale
    Arched over me a dismal gloom,
While all God's sun-lit waves rolled by,
    And left me deepening down to doom.

I saw the opening maw of hell,
    With endless pains and sorrows there;
Which none but they that feel can tell—
    Oh, I was plunging to despair.

In black distress, I called my God,
    When I could scarcely believe him mine,
He bowed his ear to my complaints—
    No more the whale did me confine.

With speed he flew to my relief,
    As on a radiant dolphin borne;
Awful, yet bright, as lightning shone
    The face of my Deliverer God.

My song for ever shall record
    That terrible, that joyful hour;
I give the glory to my God,
    His all the mercy and the power.

(from *Moby Dick*)

*Herman Melville (1819–1891) was the American novelist
and poet who wrote* Moby Dick.

JOHN MILTON

They Serve Him Best

When I consider how my light is spent,
    Ere half my days, in this dark world and wide,
    And that one talent which is death to hide
    Lodged with me useless, though my soul more bent
To serve therewith my Maker, and present
    My true account, lest he returning chide,
    "Doth God exact day-labour, light denied?"
    I fondly ask. But Patience, to prevent
That murmur, soon replies: "God doth not need
    Either man's work or his own gifts; who best
    Bear his mild yoke, they serve him best. His state
Is kingly: thousands at his bidding speed,
    And post o'er land and ocean without rest;
    They also serve who only stand and wait."

(on Milton's blindness)

The Hymn

It was the winter-wild,
While the heaven-born Child,
All meanly wrapt in the rude manger lies;

Nature in awe to Him
Had doff'd her gaudy trim,
With her great Master so to sympathize:
It was no season then for her
To wanton with the sun, her lusty paramour.
Only with speeches fair
She woos the gentle air
To hide her guilty front with innocent snow;
And on her naked shame,
Pollute with sinful blame,
The saintly veil of maiden white to throw;
Confounded, that her Maker's eyes
Should look so near upon her foul deformities.
But He, her fears to cease,
Sent down the meek-eyed Peace;
She, crown'd with olive-green, came softly sliding
Down through the turning sphere,
His ready harbinger,
With turtle wing the amorous clouds dividing,
And waving wide her myrtle wand,
She strikes a universal peace through sea and land.
But peaceful was the night
Wherein the Prince of Light
His reign of peace upon the earth began:
The winds, with wonder whist,
Smoothly the waters kist,
Whispering new joys to the mild ocean—
Who now hath quite forgot to rave,
While birds of calm sit brooding on the charmèd
wave.

*John Milton (1608–1674) was the British poet
who wrote* Paradise Lost.

THOMAS MORE

Give Me, Good Lord

GLORIOUS GOD, give me grace to amend my life, and to have an eye to my end without begrudging death, which to those who die in you, good Lord, is the gate of a wealthy life.

And give me, good Lord, a humble, lowly, quiet, peaceable, patient, charitable, kind, tender and pitiful mind, in all my works and all my words and all my thoughts, to have a taste of your holy, blessed Spirit.

Give me, good Lord, a full faith, a firm hope, and a fervent charity, a love of you incomparably above the love of myself.

Give me, good Lord, a longing to be with you, not to avoid the calamities of this world, nor so much to attain the joys of heaven, as simply for love of you.

And give me, good Lord, your love and favour, which my love of you, however great it might be, could not deserve were it not for your great goodness.

These things, good Lord, that I pray for, give me your grace to labour for.

(written a week before his execution)

Tender, Loving Father

Grant, I thee pray, such heat into mine heart
That to this love of thine may be equal;
Grant me from Satan's service to astart,
With whom me rueth so long to have been thrall;
Grant me, good Lord and Creator of all,
The flame to quench of all sinful desire
And in thy love set all mine heart afire.

That when the journey of this deadly life
My silly ghost hath finished, and thence
Departen must without his fleshly wife,
Alone into his Lord's high presence,
He may thee find, O well of indulgence,
In thy lordship not as a lord, but rather
As a very tender, loving father.

*Thomas More (1478–1535) was the English cleric
and statesman who wrote* Utopia.

JOHN MUIR

Heaven's Light

As soon as I got out into Heaven's light I started on another long excursion, making haste with all my heart to store my mind with the Lord's beauty and thus be ready for any fate, light or dark. And it was from this time that my long continuous wanderings may be said to have fairly commenced. I bade adieu to all my mechanical inventions, determined to devote the rest of my life to the study of the inventions of God.

(upon recovering sight in his right eye,
following an industrial accident)

John Muir (1838–1914) was the American naturalist, writer, and wilderness advocate, born in Scotland.

BLAISE PASCAL

❧

Our Sins

WE DEPART from Jesus Christ only when we depart from charity. Our prayers and virtues are abominations before God if they are not the prayers and virtues of Jesus Christ. And our sins will never attract God's mercy, but rather his justice, unless they are the sins of Jesus Christ.

Conform My Will

O LORD, let me not henceforth desire health or life except to spend them for you, with you, and in you. You alone know what is good for me; do therefore what seems best to you. Give to me or take from me; conform my will to yours; and grant that with humble and perfect submission and in holy confidence I may receive the orders of your eternal providence, and may equally adore all that comes to me from you.

Great and Wretched

CONSIDER Jesus Christ in every person, and in ourselves, Jesus Christ as father in his father, Jesus Christ as brother in his brothers, Jesus Christ as poor in the poor, Jesus Christ as rich in the rich, Jesus Christ as priest and doctor in priests, Jesus Christ as sovereign in princes. For by his glory he is everything that is great, being God, and by his mortal life he is everything that is wretched and abject. That is why he took on this unhappy condition, so that he could be in every person and a model for every condition of men.

Tears of Joy

Assurance, joy, assurance, feeling, joy, peace.
God of Jesus Christ, my God and thy God.
"Thy God shall be my God."
Forgotten of the world and of all except God.
He is only found in the ways taught in the Gospel.
The sublimity of the human soul.
"Just Father, the world has not known thee,
but I have known thee."
Joy, joy, joy, tears of joy.

(from Pascal's account of a dramatic
mystical experience; the writing, wrapped
in parchment, was kept sewn
into his clothing)

*Blaise Pascal (1623–1662) was the French scientist,
mathematician, and religious philosopher.*

PLATO

Call Upon God

ALL MEN, Socrates, who have any degree of right feeling, at the beginning of every enterprise, whether small or great, always call upon God.

Plato (427–347 B.C.) was a Greek philosopher, student of Socrates and teacher of Aristotle.

EDGAR ALLAN POE

Hymn

At morn—at noon—at twilight dim—
Maria! thou hast heard my hymn!
In joy and woe—in good and ill—
Mother of God, be with me still!
When the Hours flew brightly by,
And not a cloud obscured the sky,
My soul, lest it should truant be,
Thy grace did guide to thine and thee;
Now, when storms of Fate o'ercast
Darkly my Present and my Past,
Let my Future radiant shine
With sweet hopes of thee and thine!

Edgar Allan Poe (1809–1849) was the American poet, critic, and writer of brooding mysteries.

ALEXANDER POPE

The Dying Christian to His Soul

Vital spark of heavenly flame!
Quit, O quit this mortal frame!
Trembling, hoping, lingering, flying,
O the pain, the bliss of dying!
Cease, fond Nature, cease thy strife,
And let me languish into life!

Hark! they whisper; angels say,
"Sister spirit, come away!"
What is this absorbs me quite?
Steals my senses, shuts my sight,
Drowns my spirits, draws my breath?
Tell me, my soul, can this be death?

The world recedes; it disappears!
Heaven opens on my eyes, my ears
With sounds seraphic ring.
Lend, lend your wings! I mount! I fly!
O Grave! where is thy victory?
O Death! where is thy sting!

Better Way

If I am right, thy grace impart
Still in the right to stay;
If I am wrong, O teach my heart
To find that better way!

Universal Prayer

Father of all! in every age,
  In every clime adored,
By saint, by savage, and by sage,
  Jehovah, Jove, or Lord!

Thou Great First Cause, least understood,
  Who all my sense confined
To know but this, that Thou art good,
  And that myself am blind!

Yet gave me, in this dark estate,
  To see the good from ill;
And, binding nature fast in fate,
  Left free the human will.

What conscience dictates to be done,
  Or warns me not to do,
This teach me more than hell to shun,
  That, more than heav'n pursue.

What blessings Thy free bounty gives,
  Let me not cast away;
For God is paid when man receives,
  To enjoy is to obey.

Yet not to earth's contracted span
   Thy goodness let me bound,
Or think Thee Lord alone of man,
   When thousand worlds are round.

Let not this weak, unknowing hand
   Presume Thy bolts to throw,
And deal damnation round the land
   On each I judge Thy foe.

Let it not stop when entered at the ear,
   But sink, and take deep rooting in my heart.
As the parched earth drinks rain (but grace
afford)
With such a gust will I receive Thy word.

Alexander Pope (1688–1744) was the British essayist and poet who wrote The Rape of the Lock.

CHRISTINA GEORGINA ROSSETTI

Grant Us Eyes

Lord, grant us eyes to see
Within the seed a tree,
Within the glowing egg a bird,
Within the shroud a butterfly:
Till taught by such, we see
Beyond all creatures thee,
And hearken for thy tender word
And hear it, "Fear not: it is I."

We Are Rivers

Lord, we are rivers running to thy sea,
Our waves and ripples all derived from thee:
A nothing we should have, a nothing be,
    Except for thee.

Sweet are the waters of thy shoreless sea,
Make sweet our waters that make haste to thee;
Pour in thy sweetness, that ourselves may be
    Sweetness to thee.

To the Holy Spirit

As the wind is thy symbol
so forward our goings.
As the dove
so launch us heavenwards.
As water
so purify our spirits.
As a cloud
so abate our temptations.
As dew
so revive our languor.
As fire
So purge out our dross.

A Better Resurrection

I have no wit, no words, no tears;
    My heart within me like a stone
Is numbed too much for hopes or fears.
    Look right, look left, I dwell alone;
I lift mine eyes, but dimmed with grief
    No everlasting hills I see;
My life is in the falling leaf:
    O Jesus quicken me.

My life is like a faded leaf,
    My harvest dwindled to a husk:
Truly my life is void and brief
    And tedious in the barren dusk;
My life is like a frozen thing,
    No bud or greenness can I see;

Yet rise it shall—the sap of Spring;
 O Jesus rise in me.

My life is like a broken bowl,
 A broken bowl that cannot hold
One drop of water for my soul
 Or cordial in the searching cold;
Cast in the fire the perished thing;
 Melt and remold it, till it be
A royal cup for Him, my King:
 O Jesus drink of me.

Give Us Grace

O LORD, give us grace, we beseech Thee, to hear and obey Thy voice which saith to every one of us, "This is the way, walk ye in it." Nevertheless, let us not hear it behind us saying, "This is the way;" but rather before us saying, "Follow me." When Thou puttest us forth, go before us; when the way is too great for us, carry us; in the darkness of death, comfort us; in the day of resurrection, satisfy us.

Make Me Pure

Lord, make me pure:
Only the pure shall see thee as thou art,
 And shall endure.
 Lord, bring me low;
For thou wert lowly in thy blessed heart:
 Lord, keep me so.

Who Shall Deliver Me?

God strengthen me to bear myself,
That heaviest weight of all to bear,
Inalienable weight of care.

All others are outside myself;
I lock my door and bar them out,
The turmoil, tedium, gad-about.

I lock my door upon myself,
And bar them out; but who shall wall
Self from myself, most loathed of all?

God harden me against myself,
This coward with pathetic voice
Who craves for ease, and rest, and joys:

Myself, arch-traitor to myself;
My hollowest friend, my deadliest foe,
My clog whatever road I go.

Yet One there is can curb myself,
Can roll the strangling load from me,
Break off the yoke and set me free.

*Christina Georgina Rossetti (1830–1894) was
the lyrical British poetess.*

DANTE GABRIEL ROSSETTI

Ave

Mother of the Fair Delight,
Thou handmaid perfect in God's sight,
Now sitting fourth beside the Three,
Thyself a woman-Trinity,
Being a daughter borne to God,
Mother of Christ from stall to rood,
And wife unto the Holy Ghost:
Oh when our need is uttermost,
Think that to such as death may strike
Thou once wert sister sisterlike!
Thou headstone of humanity,
Groundstone of the great Mystery,
Fashioned like us, yet more than we!

Soul, is it Faith, or Love, or Hope,
That lets me see her standing up
Where the light of the Throne is bright?
Unto the left, unto the right,
The cherubim, arrayed, conjoint,
Float inward to a golden point,
And from between the seraphim
The glory issues for a hymn.
O Mary Mother, be not loath

To listen, thou whom the stars clothe,
Who seëst and mayst not be seen!
Hear us at last, O Mary Queen!
Into our shadow bend thy face,
Bowing thee from the secret place,
O Mary Virgin, full of grace!

Mary's Girlhood

This is that blessèd, pre-elect
    God's Virgin. Gone is a great while, and she
    Dwelt young in Nazareth of Galilee.
Unto God's will she brought devout respect,
Profound simplicity or intellect,
    And supreme patience. From her mother's
knee
    Faithful and hopeful; wise in charity;
Strong in grave peace; in pity circumspect.
So held she through her girlhood; as it were
    An angel-watered lily, that near God
    Grows and is quiet. Till, one day at home,
She woke in her white bed, and had no fear
    At all, yet wept till sunshine, and felt awed:
    Because the fullness of the time was come.

*Dante Gabriel Rossetti (1828–1882) was the
British pre-Raphaelite painter and poet.*

Evening Clouds

Those evening clouds, that setting ray,
And beauteous tints, serve to display
Their great Creator's praise;
Then let the short-lived thing call'd man,
Whose life's comprised within a span,
To Him his homage raise.

We often praise the evening clouds,
And tints so gay and bold,
But seldom think upon our God,
Who tinged these clouds with gold.

Hymn for the Dead

That day of wrath, that dreadful day,
When heaven and earth shall pass away,
What power shall be the sinner's stay?
How shall he meet that dreadful day?

When, shriveling like a parchèd scroll,
The flaming heavens together roll;
When louder yet, and yet more dread,
Swells the high trump that wakes the dead!

O! on that day, that wrathful day,
When man to judgment wakes from clay,
Be Thou the trembling sinner's stay,
Though heaven and earth shall pass away!

Hymn to the Virgin

Ave Maria! Maiden mild!
    Listen to a maiden's prayer:
Thou canst hear though from the wild,
    Thou canst save amid despair.
Safe may we sleep beneath thy care,
    Though banished, outcast, and reviled.
Maiden! hear a maiden's prayer;
    Mother, hear a suppliant child!
        Ave Maria!

Ave Maria! undefiled!
    The flinty couch we now must share,
Shall seem with down of eider piled,
    If thy protection hover there.
The murky cavern's heavy air
    Shall breathe of balm if thou hast smiled;
Then, Maiden, hear a maiden's prayer,
    Mother, list a suppliant child!
        Ave Maria!

Ave Maria! stainless styled!
    Foul demons of the earth and air,
From this their wonted haunt exiled,
    Shall flee before thy presence fair.

We bow us to our lot of care,
  Beneath thy guidance reconciled;
Hear for a maid a maiden's prayer!
And for a father hear his child!
  Ave Maria!

Sir Walter Scott (1771–1832) was the Scottish novelist and poet who wrote The Lady of the Lake.

God's Goodness

God's goodness hath been great to thee;
Let never a day nor night unhallowed pass,
But still remember what the Lord hath done.

Mercy

The quality of mercy is not strained,
It droppeth as the gentle rain from heaven
Upon the place beneath. It is twice blessed:
It blesseth him that gives, and him that takes,
'Tis mightiest in the mightiest, it becomes
The thronéd monarch better than his crown:
His scepter shows the force of temporal power,
The attribute to awe and majesty,
Wherein doth sit the dread and fear of kings:
But mercy is above this scepter'd sway,
It is an attribute to God himself;
And earthly power doth then show likest God's,
When mercy seasons justice.

(from *Merchant of Venice*)

Adversity

Sweet are the uses of adversity,
Which, like the toad, ugly and venomous,
Wears yet a precious jewel in his head;
And this our life, exempt from public haunt,
Finds tongues in trees, books in the running
brooks,
Sermons in stone, and good in everything.

(from *As You Like It*)

*William Shakespeare (1564–1616) was the incomparable
English playwright and poet.*

Lumen de Lumine

The One remains, the many change and pass;
Heaven's light forever shines, Earth's shadows fly;
Life, like a dome of many-colored glass,
Stains the white radiance of Eternity,
Until Death tramples it to fragments. Die,
If thou wouldst be with that which thou dost
seek!
Follow where all is fled! Rome's azure sky,
Flowers, ruins, statues, music, words, are weak
The glory they transfuse with fitting truth to speak.

That Light whose smile kindles the Universe,
That Beauty in which all things work and move,
That Benediction which the eclipsing Curse
Of birth can quench not, that sustaining Love
Which through the web of being blindly wove
By man and beast and earth and air and sea,
Burns bright or dim, as each are mirrors of
The fire for which all thirst, now beams on me,
Consuming the last clouds of cold mortality.

The breath whose might I have invoked in song
Descends on me; my spirit's bark is driven
Far from the shore, far from the trembling
throng

Whose sails were never to the tempest given;
The massy earth and sphered skies are riven!
I am borne darkly, fearfully, afar;
Whilst burning through the inmost veil of
Heaven,
The soul of Adonaïs, like a star,
Beacons from the abode where the Eternal are.

*Percy Bysshe Shelley (1792–1822) was the British poet
who wrote* Prometheus Unbound.

Eternal Light

A L L - S E E I N G Light, and Eternal Life of all things, look upon my misery with Thine eye of mercy, and let Thine infinite power vouchsafe to limit out some portion of deliverance unto me, as unto Thee shall seem most convenient. But yet, O my God, I yield unto Thy will, and joyfully embrace what sorrow Thou wilt have me suffer.

Let my craving, O Lord, be accepted of Thee, since even that proceeds from Thee — let me crave even by the noblest title, which in my greatest affliction I may give myself, that I am Thy creature, and by Thy goodness (which is Thyself), that Thou wilt suffer some beam of Thy Majesty so to shine into my mind, that it may still depend confidently on Thee.

Eternal Love

Leave me, O Love, which reachest but to dust;
　　And thou, my mind, aspire to higher things;
Grow rich in that which never taketh rust;
　　Whatever fades by fading pleasure brings.
Draw in thy beams, and humble all thy might
　　To that sweet yoke where lasting freedoms be;

Which breaks the clouds and opens forth the light,
  That doth both shine and give us sight to see.
O take fast hold; let that light be thy guide
  In this small course which birth draws out to
death,
And think how evil becometh him to slide,
  Who seeketh heaven, and comes of heavenly
breath.
    Then farewell, world; thy uttermost I see;
    Eternal Love, maintain thy life in me.

Sir Philip Sidney (1554–1586) was the English
soldier, poet, and statesman.

EDMUND SPENSER

Blessed Angels

And is there care in heaven? And is there love
 In heavenly spirits to these creatures base,
 That may compassion of their evils move?
 There is; else much more wretched were the
case
 Of men than beasts; but O! th'exceeding grace
 Of highest God that loves His creatures so,
 That all His works with mercy doth embrace,
 That blessèd angels He sends to and fro,
To serve to wicked man, to serve His wicked foe!

 How oft do they their silver bowers leave
 To come to succour us that succour want!
 How oft do they with golden pinions cleave
 The flitting skies, like flying pursuivant,
 Against foul fiends to aid us militant!
 They for us fight, they watch and duly ward,
 And their bright squadrons round about us
plant;
 And all for love and nothing for reward;
O, why should Heavenly God to men have such
regard!

   (from *The Færie Queene*)

141

Love Is the Lesson

Most glorious Lord of life, that on this day,
    Didst make thy triumph over death and sin:
    and having harrowed hell, didst bring away
    captivity thence captive us to win;
This joyous day, dear Lord, with joy begin,
    and grant that we for whom thou didst die
    being with thy dear blood clean washed from
sin,
    may live forever in felicity.
And that thy love we weighing worthily,
    may likewise love thee for the same again;
    and for thy sake that all like dear didst buy,
    with love may one another entertain.
So let us love, dear Love, like as we ought,
    love is the lesson which the Lord us taught.

*Edmund Spenser (1552–1599) was the British poet
who wrote* The Faerie Queene.

ROBERT LOUIS STEVENSON

For Success

L ORD, behold our family here assembled. We thank Thee for this place in which we dwell; for the love that unites us; for the peace accorded us this day; for the hope with which we expect the morrow; for the health, the work, the food, and the bright skies, that make our lives delightful; for our friends in all parts of the earth.

Let peace abound in our small company. Purge out of every heart the lurking grudge. Give us grace and strength to forbear and to persevere. Give us the grace to accept and to forgive offenders.

Forgetful ourselves, help us to bear cheerfully the forgetfulness of others. Give us courage and gaiety and the quiet mind. Spare to us our friends, soften to us our enemies. Bless us, if it may be, in all our innocent endeavours. If it may not, give us the strength to encounter that which is to come, that we be brave in peril, constant in tribulation, temperate in wrath, and in all changes of fortune, and down to the gates of death, loyal and loving one to another.

As the clay to the potter, as the windmill to the wind, as children of their sire, we beseech of Thee this help and mercy for Christ's sake.

For Self-Forgetfulness

Lord, the creatures of thy hand, thy disinherited children, come before Thee with their incoherent wishes and regrets: Children we are, children we shall be, till our mother the earth hath fed upon our bones. Accept us, correct us, guide us, thy guilty innocents. Dry our vain tears, wipe out our vain resentments, help our yet vainer efforts. If there be any here, sulking as children will, deal with and enlighten him. Make it day about that person, so that he shall see himself and be ashamed. Make it heaven about him, Lord, by the only way to heaven, forgetfulness of self, and make it day about his neighbours, so that they shall help, not hinder him.

The Celestial Surgeon

If I have faltered more or less
In my great task of happiness;
If I have moved among my race
And shown no glorious morning face;
If beams from happy human eyes
Have moved me not; if morning skies,
Books, and my food, and summer rain
Knocked on my sullen heart in vain;
Lord, thy most pointed pleasure take
And stab my spirit broad awake;
Or, Lord, if too obdurate I,
Choose thou, before that spirit die,
A piercing pain, a killing sin,
And to my dead heart run them in.

Before a Temporary Separation

TODAY WE go forth separate, some of us to pleasure, some of us to worship, some upon duty. Go with us, our guide and angel; hold thou before us in our divided paths the mark of our low calling, still to be true to what small best we can attain to. Help us in that, our maker, the dispenser of events — thou, of the vast designs, in which we blindly labour, suffer us to be so far constant to ourselves and our beloved.

For Self-Blame

LORD, enlighten us to see the beam that is in our own eye, and blind us to the mote that is in our brother's. Let us feel our offenses with our hands, make them great and bright before us like the sun, make us eat them and drink them for our diet.

Blind us to the offenses of our beloved, cleanse them from our memories, take them out of our mouths forever. Help us at the same time with the grace of courage, that we be none of us cast down when we sit lamenting amid the ruins of our happiness or our integrity. Touch us with fire from the altar, that we may be up and doing to rebuild our city.

For the Family

HELP US to look back on the long way that Thou hast brought us, on the long days in which we have been served not according to our deserts but our desires; on the pit and the miry clay, the blackness of despair, the horror of misconduct, from which our feet have been plucked out.

For our sins forgiven or prevented, for our shame unpublished, we bless and thank Thee, O God. Help us yet again and ever. So order events, so strengthen our frailty, as that day by day we shall come before Thee with this song of gratitude, and in the end we be dismissed with honour. In their weakness and fear, the vessels of thy handiwork so pray to Thee, so praise Thee.

Robert Louis Stevenson (1850–1894) was the
Scottish novelist, poet, and essayist
who wrote Treasure Island.

Calm and Divine

Abide in me; o'ershadow by Thy love
Each half-formed purpose and dark thought of sin;
Quench, ere it rise, each selfish, low desire,
And keep my soul as Thine, calm and divine.

Mary at the Cross

O wondrous Mother! since the dawn of time
    Was ever love, was ever grief, like thine?
O highly favored in thy joy's deep flow,
    And favored even in this, thy bitterest woe!

Poor was that home in simple Nazareth
    Where, fairly growing, like some silent flower,
Last of a kingly race, unknown and lowly,
    O desert lily, passed thy childhood's hour.

The world knew not the tender, serious maiden,
    Who through deep loving years so silent grew,
Full of high thought and holy aspiration,
    Which the o'ershadowing God alone might view.

And then it came, that message from the highest,
    Such as to woman ne'er before descended,

The Almighty wings thy prayerful soul o'erspread,
   And with thy life the Life of worlds was blended.

Blest through those thirty years, when in thy dwelling
   He lived a God disguised with unknown power;
And thou his sole adorer, his best love,
   Trusting, revering, waited for his hour.

Now by that cross thou tak'st thy final station,
   And shar'st the last dark trial of thy Son;
Not with weak tears or woman's lamentation,
   But with high silent anguish like his own.

All now is darkness; and in that deep stillness
   The God-man wrestles with that mighty woe;
Hark to that cry, the rock of ages rending—
   "'Tis finished!" Mother, all is glory now!

*Harriet Beecher Stowe (1811–1896) was the American
novelist who wrote* Uncle Tom's Cabin.

ALFRED, LORD TENNYSON

Hands of Prayer

More things are wrought by prayer
Than this world dreams of. Wherefore, let thy voice
Rise like a fountain for me night and day.
For what are men better than sheep or goats
That nourish a blind life within the brain,
If, knowing God, they lift not hands of prayer
Both for themselves and those who call them friend?
For so the whole round earth is every way
Bound by gold chains about the feet of God.

(from *Morte D'Arthur*)

Speak to Him

Speak to Him thou for He hears,
and Spirit with Spirit can meet—
Closer is He than breathing,
and nearer than hands and feet.

Crossing the Bar

Sunset and evening star
    And one clear call for me!
And may there be no moaning of the bar
    When I put out to sea,

But such a tide as moving seems asleep,
    Too full for sound and foam,
When that which drew from out the boundless
deep
    Turns again home.

Twilight and evening bell,
    And after that the dark!
And may there be no sadness of farewell,
    When I embark;

For tho' from our borne of Time and Place
    The flood may bear me far,
I hope to see my Pilot face to face
    When I have crossed the bar.

We Trust

O yet we trust that somehow good
    Will be the final goal of ill,
    To pangs of nature, sins of will,
Defects of doubt, and taints of blood;

That nothing walks with aimless feet;
    That not one life shall be destroyed,

Or cast as rubbish to the void,
When God hath made the pile complete;

That not a worm is cloven in vain;
    That not a mouth with vain desire
    Is shrivelled in a fruitless fire,
Or but subserves another's gain.

Behold, we know not anything;
    I can but trust that good shall fall
    At last—far off—at last, to all,
And every winter change to spring.

So runs my dream: but what am I?
    An infant crying in the night:
    An infant crying for the light:
And with no language but a cry.

I falter where I firmly trod,
    And falling with my weight of cares
    Upon the great world's altar-stairs
That slope through darkness up to God,

I stretch lame hands of faith, and grope,
    And gather dust and chaff, and call
    To what I feel is Lord of all,
And faintly trust the larger hope.

Let Visions Come

Let visions of the night, or of the day
Come as they will; and many a time they come
Until this earth he walks on seems not earth,

This light that strikes his eyeball is not light,
This air that smites his forehead is not air,
But vision—yea his very hand and foot—
In moments when he feels he cannot die,
And knows himself no vision to himself,
Nor the high God a vision, nor that one
Who rose again; ye have seen what ye have seen.

(from *Holy Grail*)

Alfred, Lord Tennyson (1809–1892) was the British poet who wrote The Charge of the Light Brigade.

The Hound of Heaven

I fled Him, down the night and down the days;
    I fled Him, down the arches of the years;
I fled Him, down the labyrinthine ways
    Of my own mind; and in the mist of tears
I hid from Him, and under running laughter.
      Up vistaed hopes I sped;
      And shot, precipitated,
Adown Titanic glooms of chasmèd fears,
    From those strong Feet that followed, followed
after.
      But with unhurrying chase,
      And unperturbed pace
      Deliberate speed, majestic instancy,
       They beat—and a Voice beat
       More instant than the Feet—
    "All things betray thee, who betrayest Me."

Little Jesus

Little Jesus was Thou shy
Once, and just as small as I?
And what did it feel like to be

Out of Heaven and just like me?
Didst Thou sometimes think of there,
And ask where all the angels were?
I should think that I would cry
For my house all made of sky;
I would look about the air,
And wonder where the angels were;
And at waking 'twould distress me—
Not an angel there to dress me.
Hadst Thou ever any toys,
Like us little girls and boys?
And didst Thou play in Heaven with all
The Angels that were not too tall,
With stars for marbles? Did the things
Play "Can you see me?" through their wings?
And did Thy mother let Thee spoil
Thy robes with playing on our soil?
How nice to have them always new
In Heaven, because 'twas quite clean blue!

The Kingdom of God Is Within You

O world invisible, we view thee,
O world intangible, we touch thee,
O world unknowable, we know thee,
Inapprehensible, we clutch thee!

Does the fish soar to find the ocean,
The eagle plunge to find the air—
That we ask of the stars in motion
If they have rumour of thee there?

Not where the wheeling systems darken,
And our benumb'd conceiving soars!
The drift of pinions, would we hearken,
Beats at our own clay shutter'd doors.

The angels keep their ancient places;
Turn but a stone, and start a wing!
'Tis ye, 'tis your estrangèd faces,
That miss the many-splendour'd thing.

But (when so sad thou canst not sadder)
Cry; and upon thy so sore loss
Shall shine the traffic of Jacob's ladder
Pitched betwixt Heaven and Charing Cross.

Yeah, in the night, my Soul, my daughter,
Cry, clinging Heaven by the hems;
And lo, Christ walking on the water,
Not of Gennesareth, but Thames!

*Francis Thompson (1859–1907) was a
British poet of mystical imagery.*

LEO TOLSTOY

Love and Prayer

I BELIEVE in this: I believe in God, whom I understand as Spirit, as Love, as the Source of all. I believe
that he is in me and I in him . . . I believe that man's true
welfare lies in fulfilling God's will, and his will is that
men should love one another and should consequently
do to others as they wish others to do to them — of
which it is said in the Gospels that in this is the law and
the prophets.

I believe therefore that the meaning of the life of
every man is to be found only in increasing the love that
is in him; that this increase of love leads man, even in
this life, to ever greater and greater blessedness, and
after death gives him the more blessedness, and the
more love he has, and helps more than anything else
toward the establishment of the Kingdom of God on
earth: that is, to the establishment of an order of life in
which the discord, deception, and violence that now
rule will be replaced by free accord, by truth, and by the
brotherly love of one for another.

I believe that to obtain progress in love there is only one
means: prayer . . . private prayer, like the sample given us
by Jesus, consisting of the renewing and strengthening in
our consciousness of the meaning of our life and of our
complete dependence on the will of God.

Lamp of God

A WISE HEBREW proverb says, "The soul of man is the lamp of God." Man is a weak and miserable animal until the light of God burns in his soul. But when that light burns . . . man becomes the most powerful being in the world. Nor can this be otherwise, for what then acts in him is no longer *his* strength but the strength of God.

Leo Tolstoy (1828) was the Russian novelist
and philosopher who wrote War and Peace.

VOLTAIRE

My Heart

O God unrecognized, whom all thy works proclaim,
O God, hear these my final words:
If ever I have erred, 'twas searching for thy law;
My heart may go astray, but it is full of thee.

*Voltaire is the pen name of François Marie
Arouet (1694–1778), the French philosopher, novelist,
and dramatist who wrote* Candide.

WALT WHITMAN

Regions Infinite

O soul thou pleasest me, I thee,
Sailing these seas or on the hills, or waking in the
night,
Thoughts, silent thoughts, of Time and Space and
Death, like waters flowing,
Bear me indeed as through the regions infinite,
Whose air I breathe, whose ripples hear, lave me all
over,
Bathe me O God in thee, mounting to thee,
I and my soul to range in range of thee.

Cling Fast to Thee

One effort more, my altar this bleak sand;
That Thou O God my life has lighted,
With ray of light, steady, ineffable, vouchsafed of
Thee,
Light rare untellable, lighting the very light,
Beyond all signs, descriptions, languages;
For that O God, be it my latest word, here on my
knees,
Old, poor, and paralyzed, I thank Thee.

My hands, my limbs grow nerveless,
My brain feels rack'd, bewilder'd,
Let the old timbers part, I will not part,
I will cling fast to Thee O God, though the waves
buffet me,
Thee, Thee at least I know.

(from *Prayer of Columbus*)

*Walt Whitman (1819–1892) was the mystical American
poet who wrote* Leaves of Grass.

The Steps of Faith

Know well, my soul, God's hand controls
    Whate'er thou fearest;
Round him in calmest music rolls
    Whate'er thou hearest.

Nothing before, nothing behind;
    The steps of faith
Fall on the seeming void, and find
    The rock beneath.

Angels of Grief

With silence only as their benediction
    God's angels come,
Where, in the shadow of a great affliction,
    The soul sits dumb.

Yet would we say, what every heart approveth,
    Our Father's will,
Calling to him the dear ones whom he loveth,
    Is mercy still.

Not upon us or ours the solemn angel
    Hath evil wrought;

The funeral anthem is a glad evangel—
  The good die not!

God calls our loved ones, but we lose not wholly
  What he has given;
They live on earth in thought and deed as truly
  As in his heaven.

John Greenleaf Whittier (1807–1892) was the New England poet and balladeer who wrote Barbara Frietchie.

WILLIAM WORDSWORTH

The Task

And oft, when in my heart was heard
Thy timely mandate, I deferred
The task, in smoother walks to stray;
But thee I now would serve more strictly, if I may.

The Conscience

But, above all, the victory is most sure
For him, who, seeking faith by virtue, strives
To yield entire obedience to the Law
Of Conscience; Conscience reverenced and obeyed,
As God's most intimate presence in the soul,
And His most perfect image in the world.

The Virgin

Mother! Whose virgin bosom was uncrossed
With the least shade of thought to sin allied;
Woman! Above all women glorified,
Our tainted nature's solitary boast;

Purer than foam on central ocean tost;
Brighter than eastern skies at daybreak strewn
With fancied roses, than the unblemished moon
Before her wane begins on heaven's blue coast;

Thy Image falls to earth. Yet some, I ween,
Not unforgiven, the suppliant knee might bend,
As to a visible power, in which did blend
All that was mixed and reconciled in thee
Of mother's love with maiden purity,
Of high with love, celestial with terrene.

Clouds of Glory

Our birth is but a sleep and a forgetting:
The soul that rises with us, our life's star,
Hath had elsewhere its setting,
And cometh from afar;
Not in entire forgetfulness,
And not in utter nakedness,
But trailing clouds of glory do we come
From God, who is our home.

(from *Intimations of Immortality*)

*William Wordsworth (1770–1850) is the lyrical
British poet who wrote* Tintern Abbey.

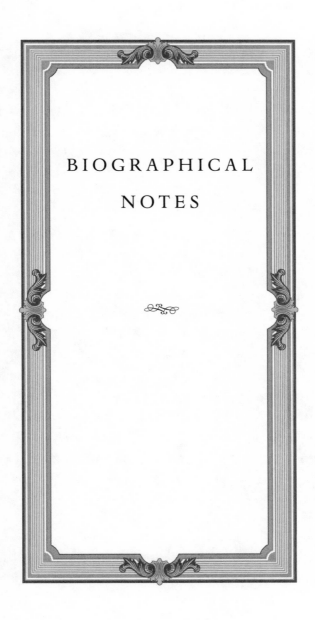

BIOGRAPHICAL
NOTES

LOUISA MAY ALCOTT (1832–1888) was one of four daughters in a household very like the one she described in *Little Women*. Her father, a philosopher, was unable to support his family, so Louisa set herself to doing so—as a housemaid, seamstress, and teacher. But her creative energies were dedicated to writing. In nature, she found a vital sense of God's presence, which she said was "never to change through forty years of life's vicissitudes, but to grow stronger for the sharp discipline of poverty and pain, sorrow, and success."

HENRY ADAMS (1838–1918), grandson of John Quincy Adams, was an American historian who studied at Harvard. Although he enjoyed a stellar reputation among scholars, his engrossing chronicle of medieval life, *Mont Saint Michel and Chartres*, appealed to a wider audience, and helped explain the animating forces behind these splendid religious monuments.

JANE AUSTEN (1775–1817) spent her early years in her father's country parsonage, a dutiful and loving daughter, surrounded by a tribe of brothers and her sister, Cassandra. Seeds of her faith were sown by her father's teaching, strengthened by private devotions and the services she attended. Her six novels sparkle with wit and piercing intelligence. Stricken with what is now believed to have been Addison's disease, Austen died painfully at forty-one, murmuring, according to Cassandra, "God grant me patience, pray for me."

WILLIAM BLAKE (1757–1827), an artist and poet, was a deeply religious, if unconventional, Christian. The lyrical and mystical elements of his imagination were intimately mingled, both reflected in his magical engravings and melodious poems. Many regard his greatest artwork to be his illustrations for the Book of Job. Blake's wife Catherine once said of him: "He is always in Paradise."

CHARLOTTE (1816–1855), EMILY (1818–1848), and ANNE BRONTË (1820-1849) were the daughters of a clergyman. Charlotte, asked at age seven by her father to name "the best book in the world," answered, "The Bible." She assisted in the education of her younger sisters, and all three read voraciously. Though they lived a quiet country life, their soaring imaginations produced an amazing literary output of novels and poems. For a time they were sent to the school for clergymen's daughters, a harsh experience chronicled by Charlotte in *Jane Eyre*. Anne—gentle, open, and submissive—wrote hymns as well as poems. Emily, who wrote *Wuthering Heights*, lived in seclusion on her beloved moors and died of tuberculosis.

ELIZABETH BARRETT BROWNING (1806–1861) was not only a devotee of literature, but a scholar of

Latin, Greek, Hebrew, French, German, and Italian. For years delicate health confined her to bed in a darkened room, where she wrote poetry to amuse herself. After these were published, through an exchange of ecstatic letters she fell in love with poet Robert Browning. They married in secret, against the wishes of her autocratic father, and fled to Italy. Their love affair is chronicled in her *Sonnets From the Portuguese*. Her poetry reflects the glory of spirituality and righteousness.

ROBERT BROWNING (1812–1889) exhibited a precocious skill at poetry, which his parents indulged and supported, allowing him to make it his profession. The main interest of his longer poems, Browning wrote, is "development of a soul." His devoted parents were Anglican, and though Browning sympathized with the spirit of their beliefs, he rejected the dogma. His marriage to Elizabeth Barrett was a legendary love story.

WILLIAM CULLEN BRYANT (1794–1878), born in a farming village in Massachusetts, was schooled in Latin by his minister uncle and in Greek by another clergyman. Two months after learning the Greek alphabet, young Bryant used it to read the New Testament. Although he studied law, he found success as an editor and journalist. His poems are remarkable for artistic and moral purity.

THOMAS CARLYLE (1795–1881), raised a Scottish Calvinist, entered Edinburgh University at thirteen, but he was distracted from divinity studies by a love for French and English literature. Later, beset by spiritual doubt, he strayed as well from Christianity. Shortly before his twenty-sixth birthday, however, Carlyle underwent a spiritual experience, of which he wrote: ". . . from this hour I incline to date my spiritual new birth."

GEOFFREY CHAUCER (1340–1400), the son of a prosperous London vintner, had a storybook-heroic youth—war prisoner in France and diplomat in the king's service in Italy. These foreign adventures exposed him to French and Italian literature, both of which profoundly affected his poetic style. His masterwork, *Canterbury Tales*, encompasses sketches of travelers on a religious pilgrimage. A committed Christian, Chaucer saw the world as a ladder ascending toward God.

SAMUEL TAYLOR COLERIDGE (1772–1834) was raised at his father's vicarage in Devonshire, England. At three he could read the Bible, and he read *The Arabian Nights* before he was five. An early plan to become a Unitarian minister was abandoned when he fell under the spell of opium (poems such as "Kubla Khan" mirror his drugged imagination). Coleridge recovered his Christian faith later in life and was esteemed a great religious thinker. He died in communion with the Church of England.

DANIEL DEFOE (1660–1731) was born into a nonconformist family, which rebelled against certain practices of the Church of England. From childhood he knew the Scriptures and copied out the five books of

Moses. He was later fined and imprisoned for vigorous articles in support of his faith. Defoe was an indefatigable writer, and his narratives—such as *Robinson Crusoe*—combine a strong sense of adventure with a forceful dose of morality.

CHARLES DICKENS (1812–1870) passed part of his childhood at his father's side in debtors' prison, and from age ten to twelve he was forced to work in a blacking factory. These distressing experiences were used later to powerful effect, particularly in his novels *Little Dorritt* and *David Copperfield*. His poignant fable of repentance, *A Christmas Carol*, has become synonymous with the season of the Nativity. Less well-known is a little volume he penned for his children, *The Life of Our Lord*. Though not averse to skewering hypocrisy in the church (or elsewhere), Dickens felt an affinity for Anglican Christianity. In his will, he commended his soul to God and the mercy of Jesus Christ.

EMILY DICKINSON (1830–1886) died in the house where she was born in Amherst, Massachusetts, a profoundly Christian New England town. After brief schooling, she settled into seclusion, probably because of an unhappy love affair, which she ended because she could not "wreck another woman's life." Almost completely withdrawn from life, Emily would not allow family and friends to publish her poetry during her lifetime. After Emily's death, her sister found more than a thousand poems hidden in boxes and drawers, some in hand-stitched booklets, others penned on the backs of old envelopes and shopping lists. These ingenious works reflect a mystical love of God. Her life was celebrated in the 1976 play, *The Belle of Amherst*.

JOHN DONNE (1572–1631) was born into a family of staunch Catholics, with two Jesuit uncles. But when he came of age, he rejected Catholicism to embrace the Anglican Church. In straitened circumstances, with a sickly wife and seven children, he was pressured by King James to take religious orders. His first sermon before the king reportedly carried his audience "to heaven, in holy raptures." His poems reflect the struggle between spirit and flesh, individual faith and general disillusionment.

FYODOR DOSTOYEVSKY (1821–1881), by vast reading, overcame a meager education. He was a promising young novelist when involvement with Russian political reformers led to his arrest. He was sentenced to be shot and was actually facing the firing squad when the czar's courier arrived, commuting the punishment to four years' hard labor. This terrifying experience, and his imprisonment in Siberia, kindled Dostoyevsky's compassion for all who suffer and made real to him the need for Christ's saving grace. His last novel, *The Brothers Karamazov*, dramatizes the search for God.

JOHN DRYDEN (1631–1700) was made Poet Laureate of England in 1668, but afterward wrote almost exclusively for the stage. Raised in a Puritan family, he attacked Roman Catholics in a play, *The Spanish Friar*. But in a spiritual turnabout, his search for what he termed an "infallible creed" ultimately led him to convert to Catholicism.

GEORGE ELIOT (1819–1880) was the pen name of English novelist Mary Ann Evans. Early and severe religious training did not dampen her spiritual idealism. She excelled at music and had an insatiable appetite for reading. At boarding school, Evans led prayer-meetings among the girls and organized charitable enterprises. In her early twenties she studied Greek and Hebrew and translated a German theologian's life of Jesus. Her novels— *Silas Marner*, *Adam Bede*, *Mill on the Floss*—are full of tributes to Christian virtue.

RALPH WALDO EMERSON (1803–1882) counted among his ancestors seven ministers, and his father led the First Unitarian Church in Boston. Emerson became a minister, but after his wife's death, he struggled with depression and chafed under rigid doctrine. His subsequent Transcendentalism, embodied in eloquent essays and poems, preaches the virtues of self-reliance, optimism, serenity, and faith in the God who dwells within. "For the soul, let redemption be sought," Emerson wrote. "Cast conformity behind you and acquaint men at first hand with Deity."

DESIDERIUS ERASMUS (1466–1536) was ordained a Roman Catholic priest in 1492. Traveling from his native Holland, he gained acclaim as the most learned teacher in Paris. A classicist, Erasmus wrote in Latin and loved literature—especially that of the

Church. He advocated a return to the source of Christianity, with its simplicity and devotion to duty. Erasmus and his times became the subject of a once-famous English historical novel, Charles Reade's *The Cloister and the Hearth*.

JOHANN WOLFGANG VON GOETHE (1749–1832) had a passion for poetry as early as age eight. At nine he built an altar and developed his own mystical religion, in hopes of approaching God directly. At thirteen he studied Hebrew and read much of the Bible, while his secular studies encompassed literature, science, law, medicine — indeed, the whole of human learning. At the University of Leipzig young Goethe wrote verses in German, French, English, and Italian. He went on to achieve such international eminence with his voluminous works that Thomas Carlyle proclaimed him "the teacher and exemplar of his age."

GEORGE HERBERT (1593–1633) was profoundly influenced by his mother, a friend of John Donne. Herbert taught briefly at Cambridge, where he had been educated. When an attempt to succeed at court failed, however, he determined "to lose himself in an humble way" and take priestly orders. He loved the Church of England and held services twice a day at his parish in Salisbury. Like his mentor, Donne, Herbert found spiritual inspiration in everyday objects. He is noted for his pious and playful poetry.

ROBERT HERRICK (1591–1674) was the son of a London goldsmith. He took a small vicarage near Devonshire and celebrated the rural customs in his village. Though his sermons were termed "florid and witty," Herrick, who never married, is far better known for his pastoral love poems.

OLIVER WENDELL HOLMES (1809–1894), a physician and professor at Harvard Medical School, abandoned medicine for poetry and prose. His father was a minister of the Congregational Church, but Holmes later turned to Unitarianism. He earned the title of "The Autocrat of the Breakfast Table" through clever essays written under that title. Holmes had briefly studied law at Harvard, but his real contribution to jurisprudence was his son, Oliver Jr., who became the greatest Supreme Court justice of his era.

GERARD MANLEY HOPKINS (1844–1889) was born into a High Anglican family, but converted to Roman Catholicism at age twenty-two. Two years later he became a Jesuit and burned many of his spiritual-sensual poems, believing the religious life incompatible with creating poetry. Fortunately, much of his innovative work survived, allowing us to experience the depth and passion of his religious convictions.

VICTOR HUGO (1802–1885) was for fifty years the greatest literary force in France. Before age six he had taught himself to read "by merely looking at the printed letters." And, at twenty-two, his literary reputation was already so great that he was made a Chevalier of the Legion of Honor. His poems and novels—the most celebrated is *Les Miserables*— exemplify the goodness of God, the triumph of life, and the power of redemption.

HELEN HUNT JACKSON (1830–1885) was born in the same year and the same town (Amherst, Massachusetts) as her friend, Emily Dickinson. Jackson, too, wrote poetry, but is best remembered for her novel, *Ramona*, about a romance between a half-Mexican girl and a Cahuilla Indian. The book, which condemns the U.S. government's ill treatment of Native Americans, was made into a movie in 1936, starring Loretta Young and Don Ameche. *Ramona* was also turned into an annual outdoor pageant, staged in the hills outside Hemet, California.

SAMUEL JOHNSON (1709–1784), an outstanding schol-ar who read Shakespeare at nine, labored seven years on his *Dictionary*. A pleasure to read, with its rich command of language and passages from poets and philosophers, the book was received enthusiastically by the English public. Johnson, however, was never able to liberate himself from poverty or ill health. His solace was God; a moving book of *Prayers and Meditations* was published posthumously. His literary legacy was further ensured by his devoted friend, James Boswell, whose *Life of Samuel Johnson* remains a biographical classic.

BEN JONSON (1573–1637), though raised by a bricklay-er stepfather, went on to receive honorary degrees from both Oxford and Cambridge. He possessed a great lyric gift ("Drink to Me Only With Thine Eyes" is one of his verses), but his real love was the theater, where he both wrote and performed (along with Shakespeare). In 1598 Jonson was arrested for killing a fellow actor in a duel, and while in prison converted to Roman Catholicism. His flirtation with Rome ended in 1610, and he returned to the Church of England. He died penniless, but was buried with honors in Westminster Abbey.

S Ø R E N   K I E R K E G A A R D (1813–1855) was a Danish philosopher and Protestant theologian who wrote on the ethical and aesthetic ideas of life. Kierkegaard rebelled against many accepted beliefs of the Danish Lutheran Church, arguing that God can be known only through faith, not reason. His writings — among them *Either-Or* and *On Christian Training* — influenced many later thinkers, especially the existentialists. Kierkegaard viewed religion as a matter for the individual soul.

J O Y C E   K I L M E R (1886–1918) was an accomplished journalist who worked for the *New York Times*, though he (not she) is chiefly remembered for his tender verse. A staunch Catholic, Kilmer found the beauty of poetry "not far from prayer and adoration." He was killed in France during World War I, attacking a German machine-gun nest.

R U D Y A R D   K I P L I N G (1865–1936) was born in Bombay and educated in English boarding schools. He returned to India at seventeen to take up journalism. Early verse made him popular, but his witty and worldly short stories, collected in *Plain Tales From the Hills*, created a literary sensation in 1890s London. "Kipling is too clever to live," was Robert Louis Stevenson's admiring verdict. Though often criticized for celebrating British imperialism, Kipling has never been neglected. His classics—like *The Jungle Books* and *Captains Courageous*—delight generation after generation. He was awarded the 1907 Nobel Prize.

C. S. LEWIS (1898–1963), an aetheist into his thirties, had a conversion experience—"surprised by joy," as he told it—in a motorcycle sidecar en route to a zoo. Lewis arrived at his destination convinced that Jesus Christ was the Son of God. For the rest of his life, while pursuing a distinguished academic career at Oxford and Cambridge, Lewis seized every opportunity to proclaim and defend what he deemed the essentials of Christianity—in essays, sermons, and radio broadcasts. Lewis's literary output includes novels of science-fiction and fantasy, poetry, and literary criticism—more that thirty books, all in print. His marriage to Joy Davidman Gresham was dramatized in a 1993 movie, *Shadowlands*, starring Anthony Hopkins and Debra Winger.

CHARLES LAMB (1775–1834) labored for thirty-three years as an accountant in the East India House, but what he called his "true works" were poems, essays, and criticisms. In 1796 his sister Mary, in a manic state, stabbed their mother to death. Rather than have Mary incarcerated in an asylum, Charles took charge of her in what became a lifelong commitment. Together they wrote *Tales Founded on the Plays of Shakespeare* and *Poetry for Children*.

HERMAN MELVILLE (1819–1891) settled down to a comfortable life as a customs inspector on the New York docks in 1866—after a wildly adventurous youth. At age eighteen he had run away to sea. In the course of a whaling cruise in the Pacific, he was captured by cannibals in the Marquesas, then rescued by an Australian ship, which he left at Tahiti. Fortunately for posterity, Melville devoted the final twenty-five years of his life to literature. His masterpiece, *Moby Dick*, which was dedicated to his dear friend, Nathaniel Hawthorne, portrays seafaring life with an unmatched vigor and originality.

JOHN MILTON (1608–1674) entered Cambridge with the idea of becoming a clergyman, but abandoned it because, he wrote, "tyranny had invaded" the Church of England. He afterward devoted himself to scholarship and literature. Though profoundly religious and a genuine Christian who valued (and studied) the Bible over all other books, Milton no longer attended church. His masterwork, *Paradise Lost,* published when he was nearly sixty, describes Satan and his fallen angels warring with God and His angelic host.

SIR THOMAS MORE (1478 – 1535), author of *Utopia,* which describes an ideal state, studied law at Oxford. As a young man, however, he longed for an ascetic life and briefly followed the discipline of a Carthusian monk—wearing a hair shirt, scourging himself, and sleeping on bare ground four hours a night. Returning to the world, he rose to become Lord High Chancellor. But More was beheaded when he refused to support Henry VIII's divorce from Queen Catherine (a conflict dramatized in the play and film, *A Man for All Seasons*). Four hundred years after his death, More was made a saint by the Roman Catholic Church.

JOHN MUIR (1838–1914) was born in Scotland and raised on a farm in Wisconsin. He was a successful inventor of factory machinery, but renounced that when an industrial accident made him fear one eye was "closed forever on all God's beauty." After sight was restored, Muir vowed to devote himself instead "to the study of the inventions of God." He began with a thousand-mile walk and continued all through life to explore and celebrate the wonders of nature. His brilliant naturalist writings led in 1890 to the establishment of Yosemite Valley as the first National Park.

BLAISE PASCAL (1623–1662) was an original genius in science and mathematics. Restricted by his father to the study of ancient languages, the boy worked out the principles of geometry on his own—and soon drew the attention of the great mathematician, René Descartes. One of Pascal's scientific discoveries became the basis for modern hydraulics. Later in life, while visiting his sister in a convent, Pascal began to seek God and found Him in a dramatic mystical experience (an account of which he kept in an amulet sewn into his clothing). Pascal, who subsequently took monastic orders, declared that perfect knowledge comes only through Christian revelation.

PLATO (428–348 B.C.) was a Greek philosopher whose ideas influenced Christian thought thousands of years after his death. His arguments on the immortality of the soul and the goodness of God profoundly affected such religious thinkers as St. Augustine.

EDGAR ALLAN POE (1809–1849), the son of actors, was orphaned at the age of three. Disappointments in love and an unconquerable attraction to liquor haunted his life and were reflected in his brooding stories. But Poe had as well a gentle, affectionate side, which appears in his idealistic, visionary poems. He died in alcoholic stupor, whispering, "Lord, help my poor soul."

ALEXANDER POPE (1688–1744) was the son of devotedly Catholic parents. He was his own tutor—not only in English, but in French, Italian, Latin, and Greek. He spent a dozen years on his famous translations of Homer's *Iliad* and *Odyssey*. At twenty-four he published a sacred poem, "Messiah." By twenty-five he was a fashionable poet and recognized wit, earning a prosperous living with his pen. His *Essay on Man* was a defense of religion on natural grounds. According to the priest who gave him the last rites, "Pope's mind was resigned and wrapt up in the love of God and man."

CHRISTINA GEORGINA ROSSETTI (1830–1894) was so devoted to her High Anglican faith that she turned down a suitor who was "either not a Christian at all, or else he was a Christian of undefined or heterodox views." Committed to the Heavenly Bridegroom, her solitary life produced a wealth of deeply spiritual creative works, marked by magical imagery, an angelic voice, and a love for nature.

DANTE GABRIEL ROSSETTI (1828–1882) was born into an impoverished but highly cultured household. His father, an eccentric professor of Italian, had highly original views on the poet Dante. The sensitive boy became a painter as well as a poet. His poetess sister Christina was the model for Rossetti's graceful painting of the Virgin Mary.

SIR WALTER SCOTT (1771–1832) read prodigiously as a child during frequent confinements due to illness. His favorite subjects were Scottish history and ballads. Scott was expected to follow his attorney father's footsteps, but his escapades at school caused his father to predict the young man would be nothing more than a "gangrel scrape-gut." On the contrary, Scott became not only a lawyer, but one of the most prolific writers in the English language.

WILLIAM SHAKESPEARE (1564–1616) was the English playwright and poet with an unsurpassed power of language. His masterful works hold up a mirror to mankind. Yet much of what we know of his life is recorded in the Stratford parish register—his birth, his marriage at eighteen, the births of his children, his death. As he looked forward to the next life, he wrote in his will: "I commend my soul into the hands of God my Creator, hoping and assuredly believing, through the only merits of Jesus Christ my Saviour, to be made partaker of life everlasting."

PERCY BYSSHE SHELLEY (1792–1822) was expelled from Oxford for circulating a pamphlet on "The

Necessity of Atheism." His rebellious notions were designed "to break through the crust of those outworn opinions on which established institutions depend." For young Shelley, that included Christianity. Yet this ethereal poet's belief in a transcendent Power caused Robert Browning to describe Shelley's verse "as a sublime fragmentary essay toward a presentiment of the corresponding of the universe to the Deity." Misjudged by the world, Shelley was a passionate believer in universal goodness.

SIR PHILIP SIDNEY (1554–1586) was born into a distinguished family and showed his brilliance at both Oxford and Cambridge. He enjoyed a successful career in court, traveled widely, turned down the crown of Poland, and sat in Parliament. Sidney's gift was poetry, and his sonnet sequence, "Astrophel and Stella," influenced many contemporary writers, even Shakespeare. During battle in the Netherlands, Sidney, only thirty-two, was fatally wounded. Dying in pain and lifting a bottle of water to his lips, he saw another thirsty soldier gazing longingly at him. Sidney passed the drink to him, saying, "Thy necessity is greater than mine."

EDMUND SPENSER (1552–1599), the son of a London clothmaker, wrote and translated verse as a boy. He possessed the supreme poetic gifts of melody, rhythm, and image, and is credited with crystallizing the forms and patterns of English verse. His masterwork, *The Faerie Queene*, is an elaborate allegory of twelve books (only six were completed), each narrating the exploits of a knight who symbolized one of the "morall vertues." Spenser was a sincere and militant Christian.

ROBERT LOUIS STEVENSON (1850–1894), to please his father, first studied engineering, then the law, but abandoned both for his real love—literature. This "shocking" decision, and the questioning of strict Scots Presbyterian theology, led his father to brand the lad a "horrible atheist." Yet spiritual concerns infuse all Stevenson's writings—polished essays and travel pieces, tender children's poetry, beloved adventures like *Dr. Jekyll and Mr. Hyde* and *Treasure Island*. Especially eloquent are the household prayers written for his family's use in Samoa.

HARRIET BEECHER STOWE (1811–1896) was, said Abraham Lincoln, "the little lady who caused this great war." Stowe's passionate belief in the abolition of slavery was expressed in *Uncle Tom's Cabin*, reflecting her deeply religious views. Her father, a strict Calvinist, headed a theological seminary in Cincinnati, Ohio, where Harriet attended school and married a professor. Five of her six brothers became ministers.

ALFRED, LORD TENNYSON (1809–1892) was the fourth of twelve children. Their father, an English clergyman, was also a skillful poet who supervised his children's schooling. Tennyson wrote verse at a precociously early age, but passed much of his young manhood in poverty and melancholy. Only at the age of forty-one, when he was appointed Poet Laureate by Queen Victoria, did his reputation and the sales of his works soar. A devout and sensitive man, Tennyson said of his wife, "The peace of God came into my life before the altar when I wedded her."

FRANCIS THOMPSON (1859–1907) was educated in the Catholic faith, studied medicine in college, failed his exams three times, and fled to London to seek his fortune. There, beset by ill health, miserably poor and lonely, he turned to opium. He was rescued by an insightful editor and found abundant consolation in religious ecstasy. Thompson wrote, "I would be the poet of the return to God." He spent his last years in Franciscan and Capuchin monasteries.

LEO TOLSTOY (1828–1910), at time of his death, was the pre-eminent man of letters in all the world. Yet, at the peak of his powers three decades before, he had renounced literature. The creator of *War and Peace* and *Anna Karenina* had spent the balance of his life in a search for moral and religious justification, not only studying the Gospels intensely, but teaching them to the village children on his country estate.

VOLTAIRE (1694–1778) said, "I wrote verses from my cradle." Though poetry was his passion, he turned his talents with dazzling effect to many literary forms—drama, poetry, novels, history, criticism, and deliciously witty correspondence—using the pen name of "Voltaire" (his real name was François Marie Arouet). As a schoolboy, he conversed with the Jesuit fathers while the other children played. Youthful satires, written while he studied law in Paris, landed him a year in the Bastille. In prison, denied pen and ink, he continued to write, committing verses to memory. His later reputation as a mocker of Christianity, however, was ill deserved. His target was intellectual tyranny; Voltaire affirmed the Deity.

WALT WHITMAN (1819–1892) was the son of a Quaker father and deeply spiritual mother. His audacious prose and poetry championed the ideals of the Transcendental period of American thought. Democracy's celebrator, Whitman believed his country's destiny was to be found in a rediscovery of the religious spirit.

JOHN GREENLEAF WHITTIER (1807–1892) was so closely connected to his faith that he was called the "Quaker Poet." Because of his staunch religious beliefs, he was a bitter enemy of slavery and used his creative energy to fuel abolition. Along with anti-slavery and pastoral New England poetry, Whittier wrote many hymns that are sung to this day.

WILLIAM WORDSWORTH (1770–1850) found his three years at Cambridge of little intellectual profit. While his family hoped he would become a minister, the thought of "vegetating on a paltry curacy" had little appeal for the young man. Yet much of his delicate and intimate poetry is absorbed with divinity—and a "communion with nature," which discovered as a child. Bereft after the death of his brother John, Wordsworth returned to the Anglican Church.

TOPICAL

INDEX